Oracle Certification Prep

Study Guide for

1Z0-147: Program with PL/SQL

Matthew Morris

Study Guide for Program with PL/SQL (Exam 1Z0-147) Rev 1.1

Copyright @ 2012 by Matthew Morris. All rights reserved. Except as permitted under the Copyright Act of 1976, no part of this publication may be reproduced or distributed in any form or by any means, or stored in a database or retrieval system, without the prior written permission of the Author.

Oracle is a registered trademark of Oracle Corporation and/or its affiliates.

Information has been obtained by the Author from sources believed to be reliable. However, because of the possibility of human or mechanical error by the sources, Author, or others, Author does not guarantee to the accuracy, adequacy, or completeness of any information included in this work and is not responsible for any error or omissions or the results obtained from the use of such information.

Oracle Corporation does not make any representations or warranties as to the accuracy, adequacy, or completeness of any information included in this work and is not responsible for any errors or omissions or the results obtained from the use of such information.

ISBN-13: 978-1478287209
ISBN-10: 1478287209

Oracle Certification Prep

Study Guide for 1Z0-147

Table of Contents

What to Expect from the Test 10

What to Expect from this Study Guide 11

Additional Study Resources 13

Overview of PL/SQL Programs 14

    Describe a PL/SQL program construct 14

    List the components of a PL/SQL block 15

    List the benefits of subprograms 16

    Describe how a stored procedure/function is invoked 17

Creating Procedures 19

    Define what a stored procedure is 19

    List the development steps for creating a procedure 19

    Create a procedure 20

    Describe the difference between formal and actual parameters 20

    List the types of parameter modes 22

    List the methods for calling a procedure with parameters 23

    Describe the DEFAULT option for parameters 24

    Create a procedure with parameters 26

    Invoke a procedure that has parameters 26

    Define a subprogram in the declarative section of a procedure 27

    Describe how exceptions are propagated 29

    Remove a procedure 31

Creating Functions 33

    Define what a stored function is 33

Create a function 34
List how a function can be invoked 35
List the advantages of user-defined functions in SQL statements 36
List where user-defined functions can be called from within an SQL statement 37
Describe the restrictions on calling functions from SQL statements 37
Remove a function 38
Describe the differences between procedures and functions 38

Managing Subprograms 40
Contrast system privileges with object privileges 40
Grant privileges 41
Contrast invokers rights with definers rights 42
Identify views in the data dictionary to manage stored objects 44

Creating Packages 48
Use DESCRIBE command to describe packages and list their possible components 48
Identify a package specification and body 48
Create packages 49
Designate a package construct as either public or private 54
Invoke a package construct 54
Use a bodiless package 56
Drop Packages 57
Identify benefits of Packages 58

More Package Concepts 59
Write packages that use the overloading feature 59
Use Forward Referencing 61
Describe errors with mutually referential subprograms 62

    Initialize variables with a one-time-only procedure 63

    Identify persistent states in package variables and cursors 65

    Identify restrictions on using Packaged functions in SQL statements ...68

    Invoke packaged functions from SQL..69

    Use PL/SQL tables and records in Packages...70

Oracle Supplied Packages 79

    Describe the benefits of Execute Immediate over DBMS_SQL for Native Dynamic SQL 79

    Identify the flow of execution..80

    Use EXECUTE IMMEDIATE..81

    Describe the use and application of some Oracle server-supplied packages 82

Manipulating Large Objects 90

    Compare and contrast LONG and large object (LOB) data types...........90

    Describe LOB data types and how they are used 90

    Differentiate between internal and external LOBs................................92

    Identify and Manage BFILEs..93

    Migrate from LONG to LOB..94

    Use the DBMS_LOB PL/SQL package 95

    Create LOB columns and populate them 98

    Perform SQL operations on LOBS 102

    Describe the use of temporary LOBs 105

Creating Database Triggers 108

    Describe the different types of triggers 108

    Describe database triggers and their uses..109

    List guidelines for designing triggers..110

    Create a DML trigger..111

List the DML trigger components 113

Describe the trigger firing sequence options 114

Use conditional predicates in a DML trigger 115

Create a row level trigger 116

Create a statement level trigger 117

Use the OLD and NEW qualifiers in a database trigger 117

Create an INSTEAD OF trigger 119

Describe the difference between stored procedures and triggers 122

Describe the trigger execution model 123

Alter a trigger status 123

Remove a trigger 125

More Trigger Concepts 126

Define what a database trigger is 126

Describe events that cause database triggers to fire 126

Create a trigger for a DDL statement 127

Create a trigger for a system event 129

Describe the functionality of the CALL statement 129

Describe the cause of a mutating table 130

List what triggers can be implemented for 133

List the privileges associated with triggers 134

View trigger information in the dictionary views 134

Managing Dependencies 136

Track procedural dependencies 136

Describe dependent objects and referenced objects 137

View dependency information in the dictionary views 138

Describe how the UTLDTREE script is used 139

Describe how the IDEPTREE and DEPTREE views are used 140

Describe a remote dependency 142

List how remote dependencies are governed 142

Describe when a remote dependency is unsuccessfully recompiled...144

Describe when a remote dependency is successfully recompiled.......144

List how to minimize dependency failures 145

Study Guide for 1Z0-147

What to Expect from the Test

The test consists of 66 multiple choice or multiple answer questions. The passing score listed on Oracle Education at this time is 77%, but as with all Oracle certification tests, they note it is subject to change. This test contains a number of questions that contain one or more exhibits.

As you would expect, in this exam you're going to be looking at a significant number of PL/SQL constructs. A reasonable percentage will ask you to look at a PL/SQL procedure, function, or package and then pick one answer from a list that is true (or false) about the construct. Other questions might ask what will happen when you invoke a subprogram or what is required in order for the subprogram to work properly.

Other items will involve questions about oracle supplied functions and packages, trigger rules and capabilities, and what can or cannot be performed using a package, procedure or function. You'll also need to recognize what PL/SQL constructs are capable of, understand how variables and parameters work, how to determine when identifiers can be referenced, and be able to differentiate between legal and illegal syntax. You need a firm grounding in PL/SQL in order to do well on the exam. You'll need to be able to parse PL/SQL in your head and work out what it does – possibly flipping back and forth between an exhibit and a question while doing so.

Read the questions completely, examine the code carefully and look at all of the answer before making your choice. That said, pay close attention to the time. With ninety minutes to answer 66 questions, you have about eighty-two seconds per question. The exhibits may not really be required to answer the question. Sometimes they will provide auxiliary information that is potentially useful to look at, but not absolutely required. The text on the exam says to look at the exhibit and then read the question, but I highly recommend doing the opposite. If you can answer a question without looking at a given exhibit, then you will have saved yourself some time. You may well need it. With a pass level set at 77%, you need to spend your time efficiently. You do not want to rush your answers, but neither do you want to run out of minutes before running out of questions. Any questions left unanswered are automatically wrong.

What to Expect from this Study Guide

This document is built around the subject matter topics that Oracle Education has indicated will appear on the 1Z0-147 exam. I've gathered together material from several Oracle documentation sources and created numerous code examples. Together they should help to familiarize you with the PL/SQL concepts, logic, and syntax that you will need to answer the questions you're likely to see on the test. Be aware that reading this guide is not going to make you into a PL/SQL programmer, nor is it supposed to. There are books available that are designed to improve your skills and knowledge as a PL/SQL developer. This guide is designed to help you to pass the 1Z0-147 certification exam.

In this book, I am assuming that you already have some experience coding in PL/SQL. If you do not, you should have at least one other source of information and more importantly, you should practice writing PL/SQL code before seeking this certification. No book, in and of itself, is a substitute for hands-on development experience. Since Oracle has made the Oracle XE version of its database free to download and use, there is no reason why anyone who wants to learn to code in PL/SQL cannot get that hands-on experience. Keep in mind, however, that this test was written against Oracle 9i, and the Oracle XE versions are either for 10G or 11G. There *are* differences. Also, when using this guide, do not simply read the text, glance at the code long enough to say to yourself 'Yep, that looks like code' and then move on to the next paragraph. The code is the meat of this exam. You must understand both the syntax and the logic of the PL/SQL functionality that will be on the exam.

The goal of this guide is to present to you the concepts and information most likely to be the subject of test questions, and to do so in a very compact format that will allow you to read through it more than once to reinforce the information. If much of the information presented in this guide is completely new to you, then you need to supplement it with other sources of study materials to gain a firm understanding of PL/SQL fundamentals. If you have a reasonable grounding in the basic concepts and are comfortable with writing PL/SQL code, then this book will help to reinforce your knowledge in the areas you will need the most. If you don't have **any** experience with PL/SQL at all, the compressed format of this guide is not likely to be the best method for learning. It is possible (barely) that it will provide you with sufficient information to pass the test, but you will have major deficiencies as a PL/SQL developer.

Additional Study Resources

The companion website to this series is www.oraclecertificationprep.com. The site contains many additional resources that can be used to study for this exam (and others). From the entry page of the website, click on the 'Exams' button, and then select the link for this test. The Exam Details page contains links to the following information sources:

- Applicable Oracle documentation.
- Third-party books relevant to the exam.
- White papers and articles on Oracle Learning Library on topics covered in the exam.
- Articles on the Web that may be useful for the exam.

The website will never link to unauthorized content such as brain dumps or illegal content such as copyrighted material made available without the consent of the author. I cannot guarantee the accuracy of the content links. While I have located the data and scanned it to ensure that it is relevant to the given exam, I did not write it and have not proofread it from a technical standpoint. The material on the Oracle Learning Library is almost certain to be completely accurate and most of the other links come from highly popular Oracle support websites and are created by experienced Oracle professionals.

I recommend that you use more than one source of study materials whenever you are preparing for a certification. Reading information presented from multiple different viewpoints can help to give you a more complete picture of any given topic. The links on the website can help you to do this. Fully understanding the information covered in this certification is not just valuable so that getting a passing score is more likely – it will also help you in your career. I guarantee that in the long run, any knowledge you gain while studying for this certification will provide more benefit to you than any piece of paper or line on your resume.

Overview of PL/SQL Programs

Describe a PL/SQL program construct

Structured Query Language (SQL) is a very powerful language with a great deal of flexibility in retrieving data from the database or inserting & manipulating data. However, SQL has no robust procedural element to allow it to apply logical processing to data retrieval or manipulation. The DECODE and CASE statements in the SQL language provide for a very basic level of conditional processing, but fall short of even moderately complex requirements.

PL/SQL adds the processing power of a procedural language to the data-manipulating capability of SQL. PL/SQL provides procedural constructs, such as conditional statements and loops that cannot be performed using standard SQL. It provides the ability to declare variables and constants, control program flow, define subprograms, and handle runtime errors. Complex problems can be broken down into discrete subprograms, which can be reused in multiple applications. SQL data manipulation language (DML) statements can be directly entered inside PL/SQL blocks, and it is possible to use subprograms to execute data definition language (DDL) and Data Control Language (DCL) statements.

Some client tools such as Oracle Forms make extensive use of PL/SQL constructs. Procedures that are created as part of an Oracle Forms or Reports Developer application are distinct from those created in the database. The general structure is the same, but they are not stored in the Oracle data dictionary. The test is about server-side PL/SQL, but there may be questions that require you to understand what client-side PL/SQL is.

PL/SQL constructs come in several different types:

- **Anonymous Blocks** – These are unnamed PL/SQL blocks. They may be executed immediately from within SQL*Plus, iSQL*Plus or a similar tool. Anonymous blocks might also be declared in-line in

an application where they should be executed. They are not stored in the database and are passed to the PL/SQL engine to be compiled and executed each time the block is run.
- **Stored Procedures** -- A procedure is a named subprogram stored in the data dictionary that performs a specific action.
- **Stored Functions** -- A function is a named subprogram stored in the data dictionary that returns a value when called.
- **Application Procedures or Functions** – Similar to stored procedures or functions, these PL/SQL constructs are stored in Oracle Forms Developer applications rather than the data dictionary.
- **Packages** -- A package is an object stored in the data dictionary that contains logically related PL/SQL types, variables, constants, subprograms, cursors, and exceptions.
- **Database Triggers** -- A trigger is a named PL/SQL unit that is stored in the database and run in response to an event that occurs in the database.
- **Application Triggers** – Application triggers are stored in an Oracle Forms Developer application and are used to respond to application events.

List the components of a PL/SQL block

A block is the basic unit of a PL/SQL program. PL/SQL blocks group related declarations and statements. The four keywords that define a PL/SQL block are: DECLARE, BEGIN, EXCEPTION, and END. They are used to make up the three sections of a block:

- **DECLARE** -- The declarative section begins with the keyword DECLARE and ends when the executable section starts. This section is optional and is used to declare variables, constants, cursors, and user-defined data types.
- **BEGIN** -- The executable section of the block starts with the BEGIN keyword and ends with the END keyword. This is the only mandatory section of a PL/SQL block and must contain at least

one statement. The executable section can contain an effectively unlimited number of PL/SQL blocks. This section contains the meat of the PL/SQL program.
- **EXCEPTION** -- The exception-handling section is used to trap and handle run-time errors. It begins with the EXCEPTION keyword and ends with the END keyword. This section is optional.

The three section keywords are not followed by a semicolon. However, the END keyword is. Also, all SQL and PL/SQL statements in the block must terminate with a semicolon.

An example of a basic PL/SQL block would be:

```
DECLARE
  v_temp    NUMBER;
BEGIN
  v_temp := 1;

EXCEPTION
  WHEN OTHERS THEN
    DBMS_OUTPUT.PUT_LINE('This block will never create an exception');
    DBMS_OUTPUT.PUT_LINE('But if one occurred, this would trap it.');
END;
```

List the benefits of subprograms

It is easier to develop and maintain reliable and reusable code through the use of subprograms. They provide the following features:

Modular -- Subprograms can be used to break a program into manageable, well-defined modules.
Simpler Application Design -- The implementation details of the subprograms can be deferred until the main program has been tested. Individual subprograms can then be added and tested one step at a time.

Maintainable -- The implementation details of a subprogram can be altered without changing its invokers. Functions and procedures improve maintainability by storing a block of logic in a single location. Any future changes to the logic only occur in that location.
Packageable -- Groups of related subprograms can be stored into packages.
Security – Subprograms allow for better control over access to database objects by non-privileged users.
Improved Performance -- Subprograms are compiled and stored in executable form. Stored subprograms run on the database server and therefore have the advantage of its power and proximity to the data. This reduces network traffic and improves response times.
Shareable -- Stored subprograms are cached and shared among users, which lowers memory requirements and invocation overhead.

Describe how a stored procedure/function is invoked

Stored procedures and functions can be called in a variety of ways from multiple different environments. They are accessible to such tools as SQL*Plus, Oracle Discoverer, Oracle Forms Developer, and other stored procedures.

- **SQL*Plus** – From SQL*Plus, most functions may be called directly through SQL statements or through the use of anonymous PL/SQL blocks. Procedures may be called using an anonymous PL.SQL block or using the EXECUTE call.

    ```
    SELECT testfunction FROM dual;

    BEGIN
      testprocedure;
    END;

    EXEC testprocedure
    ```

- **Development Tools** -- Development tools such as Forms Developer can call stored procedures and functions directly through PL/SQL using their name.

  ```
  testprocedure;
  ```

- **Another subprogram** – Stored procedures and functions may call other stored procedures and functions.

  ```
  CREATE PROCEDURE testprocedure2
  AS
  BEGIN
     testprocedure;
  END testprocedure2;
  ```

Creating Procedures

Define what a stored procedure is

A stored procedure is a subprogram that performs a specific action. A procedure invocation (or call) is a statement. Procedures must be declared and defined before they can be invoked. It is possible to declare it first and then define it later in the same block, subprogram, or package. Alternately it can be declared and defined it at the same time. Equivalent terms for a procedure declaration are a procedure specification or procedure spec. Procedures can accept parameters, update parameters and generate a return value. They are not required to do any of these. Procedures cannot be used in SQL statements.

List the development steps for creating a procedure

The specific steps for creating a procedure vary depending on the development environment being used. When creating a procedure in iSQL*Plus, the following steps could be used to create a new procedure:

1. Create a SQL script file using a text editor of your choice to define the procedure. Save the completed file in a location accessible to iSQL*Plus.
2. Use the Browse button in iSQL*Plus to locate the SQL script file in the directory where you saved it.
3. Use the Load Script button in iSQL*Plus to load the script into the buffer.
4. Press the iSQL*Plus Execute button to run the script and create the new procedure. The output from the script will display on-screen.

There are numerous other development environments where you can create stored PL/SQL procedures, including the client-based SQL*Plus, Forms Developer, and more.

Create a procedure

The basic syntax to create a procedure is:

```
CREATE [OR REPLACE] PROCEDURE procedure_name
       [(argument1   [mode1]   datatype1,
         Argument2   [mode2]   datatype2,
         ...)]
IS|AS
BEGIN
  procedure_body;
END [procedure_name];
```

If the procedure already exists in the database, you must use the (otherwise optional) OR REPLACE keywords. Below is an example of a simple PL/SQL procedure by means of the most horribly overused programming cliché known to mankind.

```
CREATE PROCEDURE not_again
AS
BEGIN
  DBMS_OUTPUT.PUT_LINE('Hello World!');
END not_again;

EXEC not_again

Hello World!
```

Describe the difference between formal and actual parameters

For procedures (or functions) that contain parameters, they are declared after the subprogram name and before the IS keyword. There will always be two classes of parameters which are defined as follows:

- **Formal parameters** -- Formal parameters are declared in the subprogram heading. For each formal parameter declaration, the name and data type of the parameter is specified, and (optionally) its mode and default value. Formal parameters can be referenced in the execution part of the subprogram by their declared names. When declaring a formal argument, only the data type should be specified when declaring an argument. The precision for a formal argument is not allowed. It is possible to use %TYPE for scalar arguments and %ROWTYPE for record arguments.
- **Actual Parameters** -- The actual parameters are specified when invoking the subprogram. These determine the values that are to be assigned to the formal parameters.

Corresponding actual and formal parameters must have compatible data types. In the example below p_empid is the formal parameter for the function GET_EMP_NAME. When the procedure is invoked by the anonymous block, v_empid is the actual parameter that gets passed.

```
CREATE FUNCTION get_emp_name (p_empid    NUMBER)
RETURN VARCHAR2
AS
  v_retval    VARCHAR2(100);
BEGIN
  SELECT first_name || ' ' || last_name
  INTO   v_retval
  FROM   hr.employees
  WHERE  employee_id = p_empid;

  RETURN v_retval;
END get_emp_name;
```

```
DECLARE
  v_empid      NUMBER          := 105;
  v_emp_name   VARCHAR2(100);
BEGIN
  v_emp_name := get_emp_name(v_empid);
  DBMS_OUTPUT.PUT_LINE(v_emp_name);
END;
```

David Austin

The compiler will implicitly convert the data type of the actual parameter to the data type of the formal parameter when required. It is good programming practice to avoid implicit data conversion whenever possible. You can do this by either declaring the variables that you intend to use as actual parameters with the same data types as their corresponding formal parameters or by explicitly converting the actual parameters to the data types of their corresponding formal parameters.

List the types of parameter modes

Formal parameters can be any of three modes. The mode of a formal parameter determines its behavior. There are three modes for parameters in PL/SQL and the mode used determines the direction in which information is passed via the parameter. The three parameter modes are:

- **IN** -- This is the default parameter mode and need not be explicitly specified. It is used to pass a value to the subprogram. Formal IN parameters act like constants – they are read-only to the subprogram. At the time that the subprogram begins, the parameter value is that of either its actual parameter or the default value of the parameter declaration. <u>Only</u> IN parameters can be initialized to a default value. The actual parameter can be a constant, initialized variable, literal, or expression.

- **OUT** -- OUT variables must be specified in the declaration of the subprogram and are used to return a value to the invoker. The formal parameter will be initialized to the default value of its type (generally NULL). When the subprogram begins, the formal parameter has its initial value regardless of the value of the actual parameter. The subprogram should assign a value to the formal parameter. The invoking process cannot assign a value to an OUT parameter – they can only be written by the subprogram.
- **IN OUT** -- IN OUT variables must be specified in the declaration of the subprogram and are used to pass an initial value to the subprogram and return an updated value to the invoker. The formal parameter acts like an initialized variable. At the start of the subprogram, its value will be that of its actual parameter. The subprogram should update its value. Only IN OUT arguments can be both read and modified.

List the methods for calling a procedure with parameters

There are two methods by which the PL/SQL compiler can pass an actual parameter to a subprogram:

- **By reference** -- When passing a value by reference, the compiler passes a pointer to the actual parameter. The actual and formal parameters refer to the same memory location.
- **By value** -- When passing a parameter by value, the compiler assigns the value of the actual parameter to the destination formal parameter. Two different memory locations will hold values for the actual and formal parameters. This is slower than passing by reference.

Describe the DEFAULT option for parameters

When declaring a formal IN parameters, it is possible to specify a default value to be used if none is supplied when the subprogram is invoked. Because a parameter with a default value can be omitted when calling the subprogram, they are also known as optional parameters. When no default value is supplied for a formal parameter, the subprogram will generate an error if it is invoked without specifying the value. Parameters without default values are therefore called required parameters. Omitting an actual parameter when invoking a subprogram will not make the formal parameter NULL unless the default is NULL. To make the value of a formal parameter NULL, specify NULL as either the default value or the actual parameter. The example below has two required parameters and one optional parameter:

```
CREATE PROCEDURE commission (p_job_id    VARCHAR2,
                             p_amount    NUMBER DEFAULT NULL,
                             p_dept_id   NUMBER)
IS
BEGIN
  UPDATE hr.employees
  SET    commission_pct = p_amount
  WHERE  job_id = p_job_id
  AND    department_id = p_dept_id;
END commission;
```

Because the p_amount parameter has a default value, it is optional and does not need to be supplied in order to run the procedure. However, when a procedure is called using positional notation, there is no way to 'skip' a parameter. If the above procedure is called with only two parameters, it will generate an error:

```
BEGIN
  commission('SA_REP', 80);
END;

Error report:
ORA-06550: line 2, column 3:
PLS-00306: wrong number or types of arguments in call
           to 'COMMISSION'
ORA-06550: line 2, column 3:
PL/SQL: Statement ignored
06550. 00000 -  "line %s, column %s:\n%s"
*Cause:    Usually a PL/SQL compilation error.
*Action:
```

The procedure can be called using named notation (discussed later) with only two parameters. However, it is a better programming practice to put any optional parameters in a procedure at the end. When this is the case, the procedure can be called using positional notation with only the required parameters:

```
CREATE OR REPLACE PROCEDURE commission
                            (p_job_id    VARCHAR2,
                             p_dept_id   NUMBER,
                             p_amount    NUMBER DEFAULT NULL
)
IS
BEGIN
  UPDATE hr.employees
  SET    commission_pct = p_amount
  WHERE  job_id = p_job_id
  AND    department_id = p_dept_id;
END commission;

BEGIN
  commission('SA_REP', 80);
END;


anonymous block completed
```

Create a procedure with parameters

The following example creates a procedure that calculates the age in dog years when supplied a given birth date.

```
CREATE OR REPLACE PROCEDURE age_in_dog_years(p_birthdate
DATE)
IS
  v_dog_years    NUMBER;
BEGIN
  v_dog_years := TRUNC((SYSDATE - p_birthdate) / (365 / 7),
1);
  DBMS_OUTPUT.PUT_LINE('You are ' || v_dog_years ||
                       ' dog years old. Happy birthday');
END;
```

Invoke a procedure that has parameters

The procedure created in the previous example can be called from an anonymous block. Parameter values may be specified using the positional or the named method. The named method must be used when not all parameters are specified or when they are not specified in the same order they are declared. The named method requires the use of the "=>" operator. In the first example below, the positional method is used. Note that the call to the procedure is a statement.

```
BEGIN
  age_in_dog_years('13-APR-1974');
END;

You are 267.4 dog years old. Happy birthday
```

And no – April 13th, 1974 is not my birthday, my dog's birthday, or that of anyone I know. Alternately, the procedure could have been invoked from SQL*Plus using the EXECUTE command:

```
EXECUTE age_in_dog_years('13-APR-1974');

You are 267.4 dog years old. Happy birthday
```

The previous two examples both used positional notation to call the AGE_IN_DOG_YEARS procedure. Since that procedure only has a single parameter, named notation is somewhat redundant. When calling a procedure using named notation, the syntax is to provide the name of the formal parameter, followed by '=>' and then the actual parameter value. For an example of named notation, we'll return to the original version of the COMMISSION procedure:

```
CREATE PROCEDURE commission (p_job_id    VARCHAR2,
                             p_amount    NUMBER DEFAULT NULL,
                             p_dept_id   NUMBER)
IS
BEGIN
  UPDATE hr.employees
  SET    commission_pct = p_amount
  WHERE  job_id = p_job_id
  AND    department_id = p_dept_id;
END commission;
```

This time, however, we'll invoke the procedure with the two required parameters using named notation. Because the two actual parameters supplied are being directed to the correct 'required' formal parameters, the call succeeds:

```
BEGIN
  commission(p_job_id  => 'SA_REP',
             p_dept_id => 80);
END;


anonymous block completed
```

Define a subprogram in the declarative section of a procedure

A local subprogram (also called a nested subprogram) is created within the declaration section of a PL/SQL block. It is accessible only to the block in which it is declared. Local subprograms can be used when there is a given set of code that must be performed multiple times within a block, but has no utility outside that block. If the code might ever need to be executed from outside the procedure, then the subprogram should be written as a packaged or stand-alone procedure instead. Used properly, local subprograms can both shrink the size of the block and simplify maintenance. Local subprograms must be declared at the end of the declarative section after all local variables. The example below shows the use of a local subprogram:

```
CREATE PROCEDURE emp_years(p_emp_id    NUMBER)
AS
  v_row      hr.employees%ROWTYPE;

  FUNCTION yrs_employed(p_hiredate    DATE)
  RETURN NUMBER
  AS
  BEGIN
    RETURN TRUNC((SYSDATE - p_hiredate)/365);
  END yrs_employed;
BEGIN
  SELECT *
  INTO    v_row
  FROM    hr.employees
  WHERE   employee_id = p_emp_id;

  DBMS_OUTPUT.PUT_LINE(v_row.first_name || ' ' ||
                       v_row.last_name || ': ' ||
                       yrs_employed(v_row.hire_date) ||
                       ' years.');
END emp_years;

BEGIN
  emp_years(106);
END;

Valli Pataballa: 6 years.
```

Describe how exceptions are propagated

When an exception is raised in a procedure, the control goes to the exception section of that block (if one exists). If the exception section handles the exception, then the block terminates and control is returned to the calling program. In order to handle errors successfully, an exception must be declared and associated with the error code.

If the PL/SQL block is nested and the exception is not trapped by an exception handler in the nested block, the exception propagates. The enclosing PL/SQL block will be passed the exception. If the exception is not trapped by the enclosing block, and the enclosing block is itself nested, then it will in turn pass the exception to its enclosing block. If it is not nested, it will pass the exception to the invoker or host environment as an unhandled exception. The exception can propagate through any number of enclosing blocks (and likewise could be trapped at any level above the one where it occurred). Exceptions do not propagate across remote procedure calls.

If the exception is user-defined, then it is possible for the exception to propagate beyond its scope. If a user-defined exception propagates beyond the block that declared it, then its name does not exist. When outside its scope, a user-defined exception can only be handled with an OTHERS clause.

There are three examples below, each with two levels of nesting. In each of the examples, the most deeply nested block raises an exception. The first example traps the exception in the innermost block. The second in the outermost, and the last does not trap it at all.

```
BEGIN
  DBMS_OUTPUT.PUT_LINE('Starting Block 1');
  BEGIN
    DBMS_OUTPUT.PUT_LINE('Starting Block 2');
    DECLARE
      v_empid    NUMBER;
    BEGIN
      SELECT employee_id
      INTO   v_empid
```

```
      FROM    hr.employees;
    EXCEPTION
      WHEN TOO_MANY_ROWS THEN
        DBMS_OUTPUT.PUT_LINE('Too Many Rows');
    END;
    DBMS_OUTPUT.PUT_LINE('Ending Block 2');
  END;
  DBMS_OUTPUT.PUT_LINE('Ending Block 1');
END;

Starting Block 1
Starting Block 2
Too Many Rows
Ending Block 2
Ending Block 1


BEGIN
  DBMS_OUTPUT.PUT_LINE('Starting Block 1');
  BEGIN
    DBMS_OUTPUT.PUT_LINE('Starting Block 2');
    DECLARE
      v_empid   NUMBER;
    BEGIN
      SELECT employee_id
      INTO   v_empid
      FROM   hr.employees;
    END;
    DBMS_OUTPUT.PUT_LINE('Ending Block 2');
  END;
  DBMS_OUTPUT.PUT_LINE('Ending Block 1');
EXCEPTION
  WHEN TOO_MANY_ROWS THEN
    DBMS_OUTPUT.PUT_LINE('Too Many Rows');
END;

Starting Block 1
Starting Block 2
Too Many Rows
```

```
BEGIN
  DBMS_OUTPUT.PUT_LINE('Starting Block 1');
  BEGIN
    DBMS_OUTPUT.PUT_LINE('Starting Block 2');
    DECLARE
      v_empid   NUMBER;
    BEGIN
      SELECT employee_id
      INTO   v_empid
      FROM   hr.employees;
    END;
    DBMS_OUTPUT.PUT_LINE('Ending Block 2');
  END;
  DBMS_OUTPUT.PUT_LINE('Ending Block 1');
END;

Starting Block 1
Starting Block 2

Error report:
ORA-01422: exact fetch returns more than requested number
          of rows
ORA-06512: at line 8
01422. 00000 -  "exact fetch returns more than requested
                number of rows"
*Cause:    The number specified in exact fetch is less
           than the rows returned.
*Action:   Rewrite the query or change number of rows
           requested
```

Remove a procedure

The statement to remove a procedure is DROP procedure_name. If the procedure is in a different schema, you must prefix the procedure name with the schema name followed by a dot, and have the appropriate rights.

```
DROP PROCEDURE age_in_dog_years;

procedure AGE_IN_DOG_YEARS dropped.
```

The DROP operation is a DDL command and therefore commits implicitly. It is not possible to recover a dropped object via the ROLLBACK command. Once dropped, it can only be recovered through the use of a saved script, export or media recovery.

Creating Functions

Define what a stored function is

A stored function has the same basic structure as a stored procedure. However, the heading of a function must include a RETURN clause. This clause specifies the data type of the value that the function returns. Functions must always return a value to the invoking process.

In addition, the executable part of a function must lead to a RETURN statement for every execution path. If there is no RETURN clause in the header, PL/SQL will generate a compile time error. However, if there is no return clause in the body, or an execution path does not lead to a RETURN clause, you will not receive a compile time error. Instead you will get a run-time error if the function is executed and completes without encountering a RETURN clause.

Some rules about functions include:

- Functions can usually be invoked from within a SQL statement.
- Functions cannot be invoked in SQL statements if they return a non-server data type such as BOOLEAN.
- Functions cannot be invoked in SQL statements if they modify the database.
- Functions must be executed as part of an expression in PL/SQL.
- Functions must be invoked in the form of an expression that utilizes the return value.
- When invoked via the EXECUTE command, a host variable must be used to hold the return value.
- Functions cannot be invoked within a CHECK constraint or the DEFAULT clause of the CREATE TABLE statement.
- Functions can be invoked from within other server-side or client-side functions.

Create a function

The basic syntax to create a function is:

```
CREATE [OR REPLACE] FUNCTION function_name
     [(argument1    [mode1]    datatype1,
      Argument2    [mode2]    datatype2,
      ...)]
RETURN datatype
IS|AS
BEGIN
  function_body;
END [function_name];
```

If the function already exists in the database, you must use the (otherwise optional) OR REPLACE keywords. Like procedures, functions use formal parameters to transfer values to and from the calling environment. OUT arguments are not typically used with functions because information the RETURN statement is used for transferring data out. Arguments for a function must be declared in the header section and precede the RETURN statement. The header section is declared after the function name and before the IS keyword. Local variables are defined after the IS keyword. Functions must contain two RETURN statements. One RETURN statement must exist in the header section to specify the data type to be returned. Another RETURN statement must exist in the executable section to return the value. A function will successfully compile without a RETURN statement in the executable section, but will generate a run-time error if no value is returned on execution. This is also true if a RETURN statement exists in the executable section, but conditional logic prevents it from being reached.

The example below revisits the age_in_dog_years code that was used in the procedure example. This time the same logic is made into a function. Other than removing the DBMS_OUTPUT from the new function, the only significant differences to the code are the addition of 'RETURN NUMBER' to the heading and the RETURN clause in the execution section of the code.

```
CREATE FUNCTION age_in_dog_years(p_birthdate  DATE)
RETURN NUMBER
IS
  v_retval    NUMBER;
BEGIN
  v_retval := TRUNC((SYSDATE - p_birthdate) / (365 / 7), 1);
  RETURN v_retval;
END;
```

List how a function can be invoked

As a function, age_in_dog_years can be called from a PL/SQL block or as part of the SELECT list of a SQL statement. If called from a PL/SQL procedure, it must be called as an assignment rather than a statement.

Called from SQL:

```
SELECT 'You are ' || age_in_dog_years('13-APR-1974') ||
       ' dog years old. Happy birthday'
FROM   dual;

You are 267.5 dog years old. Happy birthday
```

Called from PL/SQL:

```
DECLARE
  v_dog_years   NUMBER;
BEGIN
  v_dog_years := age_in_dog_years('13-APR-1974');

  DBMS_OUTPUT.PUT_LINE('You are ' || v_dog_years ||
                       ' dog years old. Happy birthday');
END;

You are 267.5 dog years old. Happy birthday
```

A function can be called via the EXECUTE command of SQL*Plus, but a bind variable must be used to hold the returned value:

```
VARIABLE v_dog_years     NUMBER
EXECUTE :v_dog_years := age_in_dog_years('13-APR-1974')

PRINT v_dog_years

V_DOG_YEARS
---
267
```

List the advantages of user-defined functions in SQL statements

The ability to accept parameter-based input, perform complex processing, and then return a result provides significant advantages when applied to SQL statements. Some specific examples are:

- Can provide additional capabilities to SELECT statements for operations too complex to perform via SQL.
- Can perform complex manipulation of character strings.
- Can be used in the WHERE clause of SQL statements to provide intelligent filtering capabilities for improved performance.

```
SELECT get_emp_name(employee_id)
FROM   hr.employees
WHERE  job_id = 'AD_VP';

GET_EMP_NAME(EMPLOYEE_ID)
-------------------------
Neena Kochhar
Lex De Haan
Alexander Hunold
```

```
SELECT  employee_id, email, job_id
FROM    hr.employees
WHERE   get_emp_name(employee_id) = 'Shelli Baida';

EMPLOYEE_ID EMAIL                          JOB_ID
----------- ------------------------       ----------
        116 SBAIDA                         PU_CLERK
```

List where user-defined functions can be called from within an SQL statement

You can write user-defined functions in PL/SQL to provide functionality that is not available in SQL or built-in SQL functions. These functions can appear in a SQL statement wherever an expression can occur. Specifically, user-defined functions can be used in the following locations:

- The select list of a SELECT statement
- The condition of a WHERE clause
- CONNECT BY, START WITH, ORDER BY, and GROUP BY clauses
- The VALUES clause of an INSERT statement
- The SET clause of an UPDATE statement

Describe the restrictions on calling functions from SQL statements

In order to be invokable from SQL statements, a stored function (plus any subprograms that it invokes) must obey certain rules. These are called purity rules and are meant to control side effects. The rules are:

- When invoked from a SELECT statement or a parallelized INSERT, UPDATE, or DELETE statement, the subprogram cannot modify any database tables.
- When invoked from an INSERT, UPDATE, or DELETE statement, the subprogram cannot query or modify any database tables modified by that statement.
- When invoked from a SELECT, INSERT, UPDATE, or DELETE statement, the subprogram cannot execute any of the following

SQL statements, unless PRAGMA AUTONOMOUS_TRANSACTION is specified:
- ✓ Transaction control statements (such as COMMIT)
- ✓ Session control statements (such as SET ROLE)
- ✓ System control statements (such as ALTER SYSTEM)
- ✓ Database definition language (DDL) statements (such as CREATE), which are committed automatically

Remove a function

As with procedures, the DROP command is used to permanently drop a function:

```
DROP FUNCTION age_in_dog_years;

function AGE_IN_DOG_YEARS dropped.
```

The DROP operation is a DDL command and therefore commits implicitly. It is not possible to recover a dropped object via the ROLLBACK command. Once dropped, it can only be recovered through the use of a saved script, export or media recovery.

Describe the differences between procedures and functions

A PL/SQL function has the same basic structure as a procedure. However, there are several differences in how they are constructed and used:

- A function heading must include a RETURN clause that specifies the type of data returned by the function. A procedure <u>cannot</u> have a return clause in the heading.
- A function must have a RETURN statement in the executable section of the block. Procedures **can** have a return statement in the execution block, but this is both optional and not recommended.

- Procedures are invoked as a statement whereas functions are invoked as an expression (i.e. a variable is assigned to the return value of the function, or a value in a SQL statement is assigned the return value of the function).
- As a general rule, procedures are used to perform an action whereas a function is used to compute a value.

Managing Subprograms

Contrast system privileges with object privileges

There are two broad classes of privileges that can be granted to a user or role:

- **System Privileges** – Provide the ability to perform a task that has a scope beyond that of a single database object. There are a number of Oracle system privileges, but the ones relevant to PL/SQL will be ones with either CREATE or ANY in the privilege being granted. When system privileges are granted with the ANY keyword, they have a scope of the entire database, for example DROP ANY PROCEDURE. Without the ANY clause, they have a scope that is just for the schema of the user who has been granted the privilege, for example CREATE PROCEDURE.
- **Object Privileges** – Provide the ability to perform a task on a specific database object. The only object privilege applicable to PL/SQL objects is EXECUTE. Users always have execute privileges on PL/SQL objects in their own schema, so object privilege grants will always be directed at a PL/SQL objects in a different schema.

The PL/SQL system privileges follow (note that the PROCEDURE privileges apply to FUNCTION and PACKAGE rights as well):
- **CREATE PROCEDURE** -- Allows a user to create a PL/SQL procedure, function or package owned by that user.
- **CREATE ANY PROCEDURE** -- Allows a user to create a PL/SQL procedure, function or package owned by any user in the database.
- **EXECUTE ANY PROCEDURE** – Allows a user to execute any PL/SQL procedure, function or package in the database.
- **ALTER ANY PROCEDURE** – Allows a user to alter any PL/SQL procedure, function or package in the database.
- **DROP ANY PROCEDURE** -- Allows a user to drop any PL/SQL procedure, function or package in the database.

The only PL/SQL Object Privileges is:
- **EXECUTE** – Allows a user to execute a PL/SQL package, procedure or function in another schema directly.

Grant privileges

System privileges are always granted by privileged users (i.e. DBAs). Granting database users the ability to create objects and **especially** granting them the ability to make changes to objects in other schemas is not something to be done without a defined need.

If you have a privileged database developer, you might grant them the rights to create, alter, and drop PL/SQL objects throughout the database.

```
GRANT CREATE ANY PROCEDURE to ocpguru;
GRANT ALTER ANY PROCEDURE to ocpguru;
GRANT DROP ANY PROCEDURE to ocpguru;
```

Unless you are the owner of a PL/SQL construct or have the system privilege EXECUTE ANY PROCEDURE, you must be granted the EXECUTE privilege to run it. By default, the executor only requires the EXECUTE privilege and does not require privileges for any objects referenced in the construct. If the subprogram has the AUTHID CURRENT_USER clause in the header, then the executor will require privileges on any referenced objects.

Object privileges are much less powerful and can be granted by the owner of the PL/SQL objects. Since the object cannot be changed, only invoked, the execute privilege can be granted more freely. For example, the HR schema might be granted the EXECUTE privilege on the procedure EMP_YEARS with the following grant:

```
GRANT EXECUTE ON ocpguru.emp_years TO hr;

GRANT succeeded.
```

Privileges that have been granted can be removed using the REVOKE statement:

```
REVOKE EXECUTE ON ocpguru.emp_years FROM hr;

REVOKE succeeded.
```

Contrast invokers rights with definers rights

By default, subprograms execute with the privileges of their owners. This allows indirect access to database objects and more granular data security. Users only need to be granted the privilege to execute the procedure and not privileges on the objects accessed by the subprogram. The AUTHID property of a stored PL/SQL unit determines the authorization under which a PL/SQL subprogram operates at run-time. This affects the name resolution and privilege checking when it issues SQL statements. The AUTHID property has no effect on compilation of the subprogram. For stored PL/SQL units that you create with the following statements, you can use the clause to specify either DEFINER (the default) or CURRENT_USER:

- **CREATE FUNCTION name RETURN type AUTHID CURRENT_USER...**
- **CREATE PACKAGE name AUTHID CURRENT_USER...**
- **CREATE PROCEDURE name AUTHID CURRENT_USER...**

The two options for authorization are:

- **CURRENT_USER** -- When AUTHID is set to CURRENT_USER, the unit is called an invoker's rights unit, or IR unit. When the PL/SQL subprogram is executed, it will run using the rights of the person that invoked the code, not the person who created it.
- **DEFINER** -- When AUTHID is set to DEFINER, the unit is called a definer's rights unit, or DR unit. When the PL/SQL subprogram is executed, it will run using the rights of the person that created the code, not the person who invoked it. A trigger or view always behaves like a DR unit.

In practice, using definer's rights allows you to provide the schema executing a PL/SQL object indirect access to objects they might not be able to access directly. For example, a procedure written by a schema with access to the HR.EMPLOYEES table is created with DEFINER rights.

Privileges to execute that procedure are then granted to a second user that does not have access to HR.EMPLOYEES. The second user has been given indirect access to that table. This can be a good thing or a bad thing, depending on the intent. Creating that same procedure with INVOKER rights will prevent the second user from accessing the HR.EMPLOYEES table.

In the below example, the procedure get_employee_salary will return the salary when supplied with an employee ID. Since the AUTHID clause is not included, the procedure is created with DEFINER's rights by default. If execute is granted on this function to any other schema, they will be able to get salary data regardless of whether they otherwise have access to the HR.EMPLOYEES table.

```
CREATE PROCEDURE get_employee_sal(p_empid    NUMBER)
IS
  v_SQL    VARCHAR2(200);
  v_row    hr.employees%ROWTYPE;
BEGIN
  v_SQL := 'SELECT * FROM hr.employees WHERE ' ||
           'employee_id = ' || p_empid;

  EXECUTE IMMEDIATE v_SQL INTO v_row;

  DBMS_OUTPUT.PUT_LINE('Salary for ' || v_row.first_name ||
                       ' ' || v_row.last_name ||
                       ' is ' || v_row.salary);
END get_employee_sal;


EXECUTE get_employee_sal(106)

Salary for Valli Pataballa is 4800
```

If the same function is instead created with the AUTHID CURRENT_USER clause, then any schemas granted execute privileges on the function will only be able to get salary data if they have SELECT access to the HR_EMPLOYEES table granted to them.

```
CREATE OR REPLACE PROCEDURE get_employee_sal(p_empid
NUMBER)
AUTHID CURRENT_USER
IS
  v_SQL    VARCHAR2(200);
  v_row    hr.employees%ROWTYPE;
BEGIN
  v_SQL := 'SELECT * FROM hr.employees WHERE ' ||
          'employee_id = ' || p_empid;

  EXECUTE IMMEDIATE v_SQL INTO v_row;

  DBMS_OUTPUT.PUT_LINE('Salary for ' || v_row.first_name ||
                       ' ' || v_row.last_name ||
                       ' is ' || v_row.salary);
END get_employee_sal;
```

Identify views in the data dictionary to manage stored objects

There are several data dictionary views that you can use to get information about stored PL/SQL objects. The three most commonly used are the *_OBJECTS, *_SOURCE, and *_ERRORS views. Information about each of the three follows:

ALL_OBJECTS -- Describes all objects accessible to the current user. The related views DBA_OBJECTS and USER_OBJECTS display all objects in the database and all objects owned by the current user respectively. Some of the columns available in this view follow (OWNER does not appear in the USER version of this view):

- **OWNER** -- Owner of the object
- **OBJECT_NAME** -- Name of the object
- **OBJECT_ID** -- Dictionary object number of the object
- **OBJECT_TYPE** -- Type of the object (such as TABLE, INDEX)
- **CREATED** -- Timestamp for the creation of the object

- **LAST_DDL_TIME** -- Timestamp for the last modification of the object resulting from a DDL statement (including grants and revokes)
- **TIMESTAMP** -- Timestamp for the specification of the object (character data)
- **STATUS** -- Status of the object (VALID | INVALID | N/A)

An example query from USER_OBJECTS that shows all objects in a given schema, their type and status would be:

```
SELECT object_name, object_type, status
FROM   user_objects
WHERE  object_type IN ('PROCEDURE', 'PACKAGE', 'FUNCTION')
ORDER BY object_name;

OBJECT_NAME          OBJECT_TYPE          STATUS
-------------------- -------------------- -------
AGE_CALC             PACKAGE              VALID
EMPS                 PACKAGE              VALID
EMPS_DS              PROCEDURE            VALID
EMP_YEARS            PROCEDURE            VALID
GET_EMPLOYEE         PROCEDURE            VALID
GET_EMPLOYEE_SAL     PROCEDURE            VALID
GET_EMP_NAME         FUNCTION             VALID
INITPKG              PACKAGE              VALID
OCA                  PACKAGE              VALID
SIMPLE_PROCEDURE     PROCEDURE            VALID
SUBMIT_TIMESHEET     PROCEDURE            VALID
TERRIBLE_CLICHE      PROCEDURE            VALID
```

ALL_SOURCE -- Describes the text source of the stored objects accessible to the current user. The related views DBA_SOURCE and USER_SOURCE describe the text source of all stored objects in the database and the stored objects owned by the current user respectively. This view does not contain the source for triggers – that is in the *_TRIGGERS view. The columns available in this view are (OWNER does not appear in the USER version of this view):

- **OWNER** -- Owner of the object
- **NAME** -- Name of the object
- **TYPE** -- Type of object: (FUNCTION | JAVA SOURCE | PACKAGE | PACKAGE BODY | PROCEDURE | TRIGGER | TYPE | TYPE BODY)
- **LINE** -- Line number of this line of source
- **TEXT** – Text source of the stored object

The following query pulls the source text for the procedure SUBMIT_TIMESHEET from the USER_SOURCE view. This can be useful if you have lost the script to generate a procedure and wish to recreate it.

```
SELECT  line, text
FROM    user_source
WHERE   name = 'SUBMIT_TIMESHEET'
ORDER BY line;

LINE TEXT
---- -------------------------------------------------------
   1 PROCEDURE submit_timesheet (p_ts_date DATE)
   2 IS
   3 BEGIN
   4 IF TO_CHAR(p_ts_date, 'DY') IN ('SAT', 'SUN') THEN
   5 RAISE_APPLICATION_ERROR(-20020, 'Cannot submit timesheet
                                     for weekend dates.');
   6 END IF;
   7 END;
```

ALL_ERRORS -- Describes the current errors on the stored objects accessible to the current user. The related views DBA_ERRORS and USER_ERRORS describe the current errors on all stored objects and the stored objects owned by the current user respectively. The columns available in this view follow (OWNER does not appear in the USER version of this view):

- **OWNER** -- Owner of the object
- **NAME** -- Name of the object
- **TYPE** -- Type of the object (VIEW | PROCEDURE | FUNCTION | PACKAGE | PACKAGE BODY | TRIGGER | TYPE | ...)
- **SEQUENCE** -- Sequence number (for ordering purposes)
- **LINE** -- Line number at which the error occurred
- **POSITION** -- Position in the line at which the error occurred
- **TEXT** -- Text of the error

If you get a compile-time error when compiling a PL/SQL object, you can use the SHOW ERRORS command from SQL*Plus to display the error information. Alternately, you can access information about the error from the USER_ERRORS view with a query similar to the example below:

```
SELECT line, position, text
FROM   user_errors
WHERE  name='AGE_CALC';

LINE POSITION TEXT
---- -------- ---------------------------------------------
  17       10 PLS-00103: Encountered the symbol "WILL" when
              expecting one of the following: := . ( @ % ;
```

Creating Packages

Use DESCRIBE command to describe packages and list their possible components

The DESCRIBE command (often abbreviated as DESC) can be used with packages as well as functions and procedures. When run against a package, it will list all of the subprograms visible in the package specification along with any parameters and return value data types.

```
DESC age_calc

PROCEDURE            Argument Name    Type      IN/OUT Default
---------------      --------------   --------  ------ -------
SET_LIFESPAN         P_SPECIES        VARCHAR2  IN
YEARS (FUNCTION)     <return value>   NUMBER    OUT
YEARS                P_BIRTHDATE      DATE      IN
YEARS                P_SPECIES        VARCHAR2  IN
```

Identify a package specification and body

PL/SQL packages are schema objects that allow you to group multiple procedures and functions along with any associated types, global constants, variables, cursors, and exceptions. As with named procedures and functions, packages are stored in the database in compiled form. Packages are defined in two parts, the specification and the body.

- **Package Specification** -- The specification declares public items that can be referenced from outside the package. Package specifications that do not contain cursors or subprograms can exist independently. Package specs with either of these must have an associated package body.
- **Package Body** – The body defines the code of public subprograms and the queries of public cursors. The package body can also declare and define private items that cannot be referenced from outside the package (such as variables, constants, types, and

cursors). The body can also contain initialization information that declares global variables and an exception-handling part.

Create packages

The syntax for creating a package specification is:

```
CREATE [OR REPLACE] PACKAGE package_name
IS | AS
    public type and variable declarations
    subprogram specifications
END [package_name];
```

Any types, variables, constants or subprograms declared in the package specification are visible outside the package and can be invoked by other PL/SQL constructs. Procedures and functions in a package being invoked by external constructs must use the package name as a prefix. To make a procedure or function public within a package, declare the procedure header in the specification. The header for a procedure includes the procedure name and arguments. The header for a function includes the function name, arguments and return clause. Any public variables, types or constants referenced externally must likewise be prefixed.

The syntax for creating a package body is:

```
CREATE [OR REPLACE] PACKAGE BODY package_name
IS | AS
    private type and variable declarations
    subprogram bodies
END [package_name];
```

The body of a package has a header, declaration, and an optional executable section. The executable section of a package body must be after all subprograms are declared. It is specified using the BEGIN keyword and ends with the END package_name line. Any code in this section is executed the first time the package is referenced within a session. The code will not be executed again unless the user changes sessions or the package is recompiled. Packages, unlike procedures and functions, cannot be called, parameterized, or nested.

Any types, variables or constants declared in the package body are only visible inside the package. If subprograms exist in the package body that are not declared in the package specification, then they are private and can only be referenced from inside the package.

In the example below is a sample package. For the AGE_CALC package, the age in dog years functionality has been revisited -- this time adding a bit more to the logic. The package calculates age when compared to several animal species based on average lifetimes. The package has a function called YEARS that performs the age calculation using a human lifespan of 70 years and an animal lifespan that is set by a second procedure called SET_LIFESPAN. The animal lifespan is stored in a private package variable named l_animal and the human lifespan in a private package constant named l_human.

```
CREATE PACKAGE age_calc
AS
   FUNCTION years(p_birthdate   DATE,
                  p_species     VARCHAR2)
   RETURN NUMBER;

   PROCEDURE set_lifespan(p_species    VARCHAR2);

END age_calc;


CREATE PACKAGE BODY age_calc
AS
   l_human    CONSTANT NUMBER    := 70;
   l_animal   NUMBER;

   FUNCTION years(p_birthdate   DATE,
                  p_species     VARCHAR2)
   RETURN NUMBER
   IS
      v_retval   NUMBER;
```

```
  BEGIN
    set_lifespan(p_species);
    v_retval := TRUNC((SYSDATE - p_birthdate) /
                      (365 / (l_human / l_animal)), 1);
    RETURN v_retval;

  END years;


  PROCEDURE set_lifespan(p_species    VARCHAR2)
  IS
  BEGIN
    CASE p_species
      WHEN 'Galapagos tortoise' THEN
        l_animal := 200;
      WHEN 'Carp' THEN
        l_animal := 100;
      WHEN 'Gray Whale' THEN
        l_animal := 70;
      WHEN 'Alligator' THEN
        l_animal := 50;
      WHEN 'Elephant' THEN
        l_animal := 35;
      WHEN 'Dolphin' THEN
        l_animal := 30;
      WHEN 'Snake' THEN
        l_animal := 20;
      WHEN 'Black Bear' THEN
        l_animal := 18;
      WHEN 'Tiger' THEN
        l_animal := 16;
      ELSE
        l_animal := l_human;
    END CASE;
  END set_lifespan;

END age_calc;
```

Create related Variables, Constants, Cursors, Exceptions, Procedures, and Functions

Variables, Constants, Cursors, Exceptions, Procedures, and functions are all constructs that can be declared in a package specification or package body. Note that triggers are not in that list. Database and application triggers are constructs that cannot be part of a package. For any of the constructs defined in a package – if they are in the package specification, then the construct is public and can be referenced from outside the package. If declared within the package body, then they are private and can only be referenced from within the package.

The AGE_CALG package shown above already has most of the elements listed for this section. The only elements missing are exceptions and cursors. A modified version of the package below creates a table to hold the animals and their ages. This allows the use of a cursor to locate the lifespan of the animal rather than a CASE statement. A user-defined exception is defined for cases where the animal does not exist in the table. The variables, constants, cursor, and exception are all defined in the package body and as such are private. A new variable has been added to hold the lifespan of humans: g_human. Because this variable is defined in the package specification, it is public. The 'g_' prefix is my standard for specifying a global (public) package variable vs. 'l_' for a local (private) package variable. The code in the package is set up such that if no value is supplied for g_human, the value from the constant l_human will be used for the calculation.

```
CREATE TABLE animal_lifespans (
animal_name    VARCHAR2(40),
lifespan       NUMBER);

INSERT INTO animal_lifespans VALUES ('Galapagos tortoise', 200);
INSERT INTO animal_lifespans VALUES ('Carp', 100);
INSERT INTO animal_lifespans VALUES ('Gray Whale', 70);
INSERT INTO animal_lifespans VALUES ('Alligator', 50);
INSERT INTO animal_lifespans VALUES ('Elephant', 35);
INSERT INTO animal_lifespans VALUES ('Dolphin', 30);
INSERT INTO animal_lifespans VALUES ('Snake', 20);
INSERT INTO animal_lifespans VALUES ('Black Bear', 18);
INSERT INTO animal_lifespans VALUES ('Tiger', 16);


CREATE OR REPLACE PACKAGE age_calc
AS
```

```
  g_human         NUMBER;
  FUNCTION years(p_birthdate  DATE,
                 p_species    VARCHAR2)
  RETURN NUMBER;

  PROCEDURE set_lifespan(p_species   VARCHAR2);

END age_calc;


CREATE OR REPLACE PACKAGE BODY age_calc
AS
  l_human         CONSTANT NUMBER   := 70;
  l_animal        NUMBER;
  l_animal_name   animal_lifespans.animal_name%TYPE;

  CURSOR c_lifespan IS
    SELECT lifespan
    FROM   animal_lifespans
    WHERE  animal_name = l_animal_name;

  x_invalid_animal    EXCEPTION;
  PRAGMA EXCEPTION_INIT(x_invalid_animal, -20021);


  FUNCTION years(p_birthdate  DATE,
                 p_species    VARCHAR2)
  RETURN NUMBER
  IS
    v_retval   NUMBER;
  BEGIN
    set_lifespan(p_species);
    v_retval := TRUNC((SYSDATE - p_birthdate) /
                     (365 / (NVL(g_human, l_human) /
                     l_animal)), 1);
    RETURN v_retval;

  END years;


  PROCEDURE set_lifespan(p_species    VARCHAR2)
  IS
  BEGIN
    l_animal := NULL;
    l_animal_name := p_species;
```

```
   FOR v_Lp IN c_lifespan LOOP
     l_animal := v_Lp.lifespan;
   END LOOP;

   IF l_animal IS NULL THEN
     RAISE x_invalid_animal;
   END IF;
 END set_lifespan;

END age_calc;
```

Designate a package construct as either public or private

- **Public Constructs** -- Any package constructs that are declared in the package specification are public. The constructs are visible and accessible in the package as well as outside of the package.
- **Private Constructs** -- Any package constructs that are declared in the package body rather than the package specification are private. The constructs are visible and accessible in the package but are not visible or accessible outside of the package.

This is a really short section, but it is a really easy concept. If a package construct (be it variable, exception, subprogram, TYPE, etc) is declared in the package specification, then it is public and can be referenced from outside the package. If a construct is declared only in the package body, then it is private and can only be referenced from inside the package.

Invoke a package construct

The YEARS function in the AGE_CALC package created earlier can be called from a SELECT statement. The first two examples below call the function for different animals.

```
SELECT age_calc.years('13-APR-1974','Galapagos tortoise') AS
AGE
FROM    dual;

AGE
---
13.3

SELECT age_calc.years('13-APR-1974','Dolphin') AS AGE
FROM    dual;

AGE
---
89.1
```

The function can also be called from a PL/SQL block, as the example below demonstrates:

```
DECLARE
  v_years    NUMBER;
  v_animal   VARCHAR2(20) := 'Alligator';
BEGIN
  v_years := age_calc.years('13-APR-1974', v_animal);

  DBMS_OUTPUT.PUT_LINE('You are ' || v_years ||
                       ' ' || v_animal ||
                       ' years old. Happy birthday');
END;

You are 53.5 Alligator years old. Happy birthday
```

So far we have not made use of the g_human variable. So far the default human lifespan of 70 years has been used. The example below is identical to the previous one except that it will specify a value for AGE_CALC.G_HUMAN. Specifying the variable changes the returned age from 53.5 to 61.2.:

```
DECLARE
  v_years    NUMBER;
  v_animal   VARCHAR2(20) := 'Alligator';
BEGIN
  age_calc.g_human = 80;
  v_years := age_calc.years('13-APR-1974', v_animal);

  DBMS_OUTPUT.PUT_LINE('You are ' || v_years ||
                       ' ' || v_animal ||
                       ' years old. Happy birthday');
END;

You are 61.2 Alligator years old. Happy birthday
```

If the function is called with an animal name that does not exist in the ANIMAL_LIFESPANS table, then the error 20021 is raised:

```
SELECT age_calc.years('13-APR-1974','Ferret') AS AGE
FROM   dual;

ORA-20021:
ORA-06512: at "OCPGURU.AGE_CALC", line 40
ORA-06512: at "OCPGURU.AGE_CALC", line 22
```

Use a bodiless package

If a package specification does not contain any subprogram or cursor declarations, there is no need for a package body. Bodiless packages are sometimes used for standardizing constants and exceptions. This allows the use of a consistent set of exceptions and constants to be used across all of the code implemented in a given database. If there are any changes to these values, then they need be made in only a single location, considerably simplifying maintenance requirements.

```
CREATE PACKAGE std_names
AS
  c_domain         CONSTANT    VARCHAR2(100) := 'thiscompany.com';
  c_serverip       CONSTANT    VARCHAR2(20)  := '10.10.10.10';
  c_smtp_server    CONSTANT    VARCHAR2(20)  := '10.10.10.11';
  c_err_notice     CONSTANT    VARCHAR2(100) := 'dba@comp.com';

  x_snapshot_too_old     EXCEPTION;
  PRAGMA EXCEPTION_INIT(x_snapshot_too_old, -1555);

END std_names;
```

The code below looks for the defined exception X_SNAPSHOT_TOO_OLD and sends email to the address defined in the STD_NAMES package specification as the destination for error notices:

```
PROCEDURE anyproc
AS
BEGIN
...
EXCEPTION
  WHEN std_names.x_snapshot_too_old THEN
    email_pkg.send_mail(std_names.c_err_notice, 'Error in anyproc: ' || SQLERRM);
END anyproc;
```

Drop Packages

The DROP command can be used to drop a package. You can drop the package body only, or both the package body and the spec. You cannot drop **just** the package specification when a package body exists. If you drop a package specification and a package body exists, then it is dropped as well.

```
DROP PACKAGE BODY age_calc;

package body AGE_CALC dropped.
```

```
DROP PACKAGE age_calc;

package AGE_CALC dropped.
```

Identify benefits of Packages

Packages provide many advantages, including:

- **Modularity** -- By grouping related elements in named PL/SQL modules, it is possible to distribute required application functionality into logical groupings. The interfaces between packages can be made simple and well defined.
- **Easier Application Design** -- During application design, it is possible to create only the interface information for the package specifications. Package specifications can be coded and compiled without the associated bodies. Other subprograms can be created that reference the packages, and the bodies themselves can wait until you are ready to complete the application.
- **Information Hiding** -- It is possible to share the package specification, and hide the implementation details in the package body. This allows you to change the implementation details without affecting the application interface. Users cannot develop code that depends on implementation details that might be subject to change.
- **Added Functionality** -- Public variables and cursors in a package can persist for the life of a session and be shared by all subprograms in that session.
- **Better Performance** -- A package is loaded into memory when any subprogram in it is first invoked. Subsequent invocations of other subprograms in the package use the incarnation in memory.
- **Fewer invalidations** -- When a subprogram in the body of a package is changed, the database does not recompile other subprograms that invoke it. Dependent subprograms rely only on the parameters and return value that are declared in the specification.

More Package Concepts

Write packages that use the overloading feature

Subprograms in PL/SQL can be overloaded, which means that two or more subprograms have the same name, but differences in the parameters they accept. The difference in the formal parameters can be in name, number, order, or data type family. One example of the utility of an overloaded subprogram is the SQL function TO_CHAR. When passed a parameter that is a DATE data type, the function performs a much different operation than it does when passed a parameter of a NUMBER data type. You cannot overload the following:

- Standalone subprograms
- Subprograms whose formal parameters differ only in mode (e.g. IN, OUT, or IN/OUT).
- Subprograms whose formal parameters differ only in subtype (e.g. INTEGER and REAL are both subtypes of NUMBER).
- Functions that differ only in return value data type.

The example below defines two subprograms with the same name (difference). The procedures calculate the difference between two supplied parameter values. The first calculates the difference in days between two dates. The second calculates the numeric difference between two numbers. The PL/SQL engine determines which procedure to invoke by based on the data type of the actual parameters passed.

```
CREATE PACKAGE oca
AS
   PROCEDURE difference (p_firstval    DATE,
                         p_secondval   DATE);
   PROCEDURE difference (p_firstval    NUMBER,
                         p_secondval   NUMBER);
   PROCEDURE calc;

END oca;
```

```
CREATE PACKAGE BODY oca
AS

  PROCEDURE difference (p_firstval   DATE,
                        p_secondval  DATE)
  IS
    v_retval   NUMBER;
  BEGIN
    v_retval := p_firstval - p_secondval;
    DBMS_OUTPUT.PUT_LINE('The date difference is: ' ||
                         v_retval || ' days');
  END difference;

  PROCEDURE difference (p_firstval   NUMBER,
                        p_secondval  NUMBER)
  IS
    v_retval   NUMBER;
  BEGIN
    v_retval := p_firstval - p_secondval;
    DBMS_OUTPUT.PUT_LINE('The numeric difference is: ' ||
                         v_retval);
  END difference;

  PROCEDURE calc
  IS
    v_date1   DATE;
    v_date2   DATE;

  BEGIN
    v_date1 := TO_DATE('21-JUN-12', 'DD-MON-YY');
    v_date2 := TO_DATE('21-MAY-12', 'DD-MON-YY');

    difference(v_date1, v_date2);
    difference(5, 3);
  END calc;
END oca;


BEGIN
  oca.calc;
END;

The date difference is: 31 days
The numeric difference is: 2
```

Use Forward Referencing

When a PL/SQL block contains two nested subprograms that call each other, then one of the two requires a forward declaration. It is not possible to invoke a procedure before it has been declared. If subprogram A calls subprogram B and vice versa, neither can be placed first. A forward declaration declares the subprogram, but does not define it. This allows you to declare and define the second subprogram that will call the one just declared. Finally you will define the subprogram that was declared earlier. The forward declaration and the definition must have the same subprogram heading. Forward declarations are not an issue in packages because the package specification serves to declare the subprogram. The example below demonstrates the use of forward declarations:

```
DECLARE
  v_verse    NUMBER    := 1;

  PROCEDURE tweedledum(p_param1    NUMBER);

  PROCEDURE tweedledee(p_param2    NUMBER)
  IS
  BEGIN
    CASE v_verse
      WHEN 2 THEN
        DBMS_OUTPUT.PUT_LINE('Agreed to have a battle;');
        v_verse := 3;
      WHEN 4 THEN
        DBMS_OUTPUT.PUT_LINE('Had spoiled his nice new rattle.');
        v_verse := -99;
    END CASE;

    IF v_verse != -99 THEN
      tweedledum(v_verse);
    END IF;
  END;

  PROCEDURE tweedledum(p_param1    NUMBER)
  IS
  BEGIN
    CASE v_verse
```

```
      WHEN 1 THEN
        DBMS_OUTPUT.PUT_LINE('Tweedledum and Tweedledee');
        v_verse := 2;
      WHEN 3 THEN
        DBMS_OUTPUT.PUT_LINE('For Tweedledum said
Tweedledee');
        v_verse := 4;
    END CASE;

    tweedledee (v_verse);
  END;

BEGIN
  tweedledum(v_verse);
END;

Tweedledum and Tweedledee
Agreed to have a battle;
For Tweedledum said Tweedledee
Had spoiled his nice new rattle.
```

Describe errors with mutually referential subprograms

Revisiting the nested subprograms Tweedledum and Tweedledee, if the forward declaration were removed from the previous example and the resulting block executed, the PL/SQL compiler would return an error:

```
DECLARE
  v_verse    NUMBER    := 1;

  PROCEDURE tweedledee(p_param2    NUMBER)
  IS
  BEGIN
    CASE v_verse
      WHEN 2 THEN
        DBMS_OUTPUT.PUT_LINE('Agreed to have a battle;');
        v_verse := 3;
      WHEN 4 THEN
        DBMS_OUTPUT.PUT_LINE('Had spoiled his nice new
rattle.');
        v_verse := -99;
    END CASE;
```

```
   IF v_verse != -99 THEN
     tweedledum(v_verse);
   END IF;
 END;

 PROCEDURE tweedledum(p_param1    NUMBER)
 IS
 BEGIN
   CASE v_verse
     WHEN 1 THEN
       DBMS_OUTPUT.PUT_LINE('Tweedledum and Tweedledee');
       v_verse := 2;
     WHEN 3 THEN
       DBMS_OUTPUT.PUT_LINE('For Tweedledum said
Tweedledee');
       v_verse := 4;
   END CASE;

   tweedledee (v_verse);
 END;

BEGIN
  tweedledum(v_verse);
END;
```

When the above block is executed, an ORA-00313 error is returned.

```
Error report:
ORA-06550: line 17, column 7:
PLS-00313: 'TWEEDLEDUM' not declared in this scope
ORA-06550: line 17, column 7:
PL/SQL: Statement ignored
06550. 00000 -  "line %s, column %s:\n%s"
*Cause:    Usually a PL/SQL compilation error.
*Action:
```

Initialize variables with a one-time-only procedure

The first time that a package is called by a session, the database will instantiate the package for that session. Every session that calls the package will have its own instantiation of it. Instantiation of the package involves initiation and will include all of the following actions that are applicable to the package:

- Assign initial values to public constants
- Assign initial values to public variables whose declarations specify them
- Execute the initialization part of the package body

The package initialization section is an optional component of a package body. If used, it will follow the declarative part of the package body. Typically it contains statements to initialize some or all of the package variables declared in the package. Since variables can be assigned a value at declaration, typically the initialization section is used only when the assignment logic is more complex than a simple expression. The initialization section is run only the first time a package is referenced in a session. The example below shows an initialization section used to populate two package variables:

```
CREATE PACKAGE initpkg
AS
   PROCEDURE call;
END initpkg;


CREATE PACKAGE BODY initpkg
AS
   l_invoked_by   VARCHAR2(20);
   l_invoked_on   DATE;

   PROCEDURE call
   IS
   BEGIN
     DBMS_OUTPUT.PUT_LINE('Package called by ' ||
                          l_invoked_by ||
                          ' on ' || TO_CHAR(l_invoked_on,
                          'DD-MON-YYYY'));

   END call;
```

```
BEGIN   -- initialization part starts here
  SELECT user, sysdate
  INTO   l_invoked_by, l_invoked_on
  FROM dual;

END initpkg;


BEGIN
  initpkg.call;
END;

Package called by OCPGURU on 21-JUN-2012
```

Identify persistent states in package variables and cursors

As mentioned in the previous section -- the first time that a package is called by a session, it is instantiated for that session. Part of that instantiation is setting the package state. Any variables, constants, and cursors that a package declares in <u>either</u> the specification or the body make up the package state. Every session that invokes a package will have an instantiation, and that instantiation will include the state. The package state is persistent for the life of a session with the following exceptions:

- The package body is recompiled either implicitly or explicitly.
- If any instantiated package in the session is invalidated and revalidated, then all instantiated packages may lose the package state.

Local cursors and variables declared within subprograms in a package are not part of the package state. These are persistent only during the life of any given call to that subprogram and are undefined before or after.

The following example shows the use of a PL/SQL table of records in a package. The table is declared as row of the HR.EMPLOYEES table using the %ROWTYPE attribute. In the SHOW procedure, a loop populates the PL/SQL table (index-by table) with all of the records in the EMPLOYEES table. A second loop then displays three records from that array.

```
CREATE OR REPLACE PACKAGE emps
AS
  PROCEDURE show;
END emps;

CREATE OR REPLACE PACKAGE BODY emps
AS
    TYPE t_emps IS TABLE OF hr.employees%ROWTYPE
    INDEX BY PLS_INTEGER;
    t_emp_tab    t_emps;

  PROCEDURE show
  AS
    v_ndx    PLS_INTEGER   := 1;
  BEGIN
    FOR v_Lp IN (SELECT * FROM hr.employees) LOOP
      t_emp_tab(v_ndx) := v_Lp;
      v_ndx := v_ndx + 1;
    END LOOP;

    FOR v_Lp2 IN 5..7 LOOP
       DBMS_OUTPUT.PUT_LINE('employee_id:   ' ||
t_emp_tab(v_Lp2).employee_id);
       DBMS_OUTPUT.PUT_LINE('first_name:    ' ||
t_emp_tab(v_Lp2).first_name);
       DBMS_OUTPUT.PUT_LINE('last_name:     ' ||
t_emp_tab(v_Lp2).last_name);
       DBMS_OUTPUT.PUT_LINE(' ');
    END LOOP;
  END show;

  PROCEDURE show_no_init
  AS
  BEGIN
    FOR v_Lp2 IN 12..14 LOOP
       DBMS_OUTPUT.PUT_LINE('employee_id:   ' ||
t_emp_tab(v_Lp2).employee_id);
       DBMS_OUTPUT.PUT_LINE('first_name:    ' ||
t_emp_tab(v_Lp2).first_name);
       DBMS_OUTPUT.PUT_LINE('last_name:     ' ||
t_emp_tab(v_Lp2).last_name);
```

```
      DBMS_OUTPUT.PUT_LINE(' ');
    END LOOP;
  END show_no_init;

END emps;


BEGIN
  emps.show;
END;

employee_id:    104
first_name:     Bruce
last_name:      Ernst

employee_id:    105
first_name:     David
last_name:      Austin

employee_id:    106
first_name:     Valli
last_name:      Pataballa
```

The SHOW_NO_INIT procedure does not populate the T_EMPS table. It simply executes a loop and displays records from that table. Because the table was defined in the package body, the values in it are still available as part of the persistent state of the package. The procedure then is able to access and display that data:

```
BEGIN
  emps.show_no_init;
END;

employee_id:    111
first_name:     Ismael
last_name:      Sciarra

employee_id:    112
first_name:     Jose Manuel
last_name:      Urman
```

```
employee_id:    113
first_name:     Luis
last_name:      Popp
```

Identify restrictions on using Packaged functions in SQL statements

In order to be callable from SQL statements, a stored function must obey a set of "purity" rules. These rules are meant to control side effects:

- When called from a SELECT statement or a parallelized INSERT, UPDATE, or DELETE statement, the function cannot modify any database tables.
- When called from an INSERT, UPDATE, or DELETE statement, the function cannot query or modify any database tables modified by that statement.
- When called from a SELECT, INSERT, UPDATE, or DELETE statement, the function cannot execute SQL transaction control statements, session control statements, or system control statements. It also cannot execute DDL statements because they are followed by an automatic commit.

When a function body contains one or more SQL statements that violate one of these rules, an error will be generated at run time. In order to check for rule violations at compile time rather than run-time, you can use compiler directive pragma RESTRICT_REFERENCES. This pragma verifies that a function does not read or write database tables and/or package variables. For example, the following pragma asserts that packaged function highest_pay writes no database state (WNDS) and reads no package state (RNPS):

```
CREATE PACKAGE emp_info
AS
  FUNCTION highest_pay(p_job_id    hr.employees.job_id%TYPE)
  RETURN NUMBER;

  PRAGMA RESTRICT_REFERENCES (highest_pay, WNDS, RNPS);
END emp_info;



CREATE PACKAGE BODY emp_info
AS
FUNCTION highest_pay(p_job_id    hr.employees.job_id%TYPE)
RETURN NUMBER
AS
  v_retval    NUMBER;

BEGIN
  SELECT MAX(salary)
  INTO   v_retval
  FROM   hr.employees
  WHERE  job_id = p_job_id;

  RETURN v_retval;

END highest_pay;

END emp_info;
```

Invoke packaged functions from SQL

The EMP_INFO packages compiled successfully with the RESTRICT_REFERENCES compiler directive, so the HIGHEST_PAY function is safe to call from SQL. Functions can be called from the SELECT list of a SQL statement:

```
SELECT emp_info.highest_pay('IT_PROG')
FROM   dual;

EMP_INFO.HIGHEST_PAY('IT_PROG')
-------------------------------
                           6000
```

Functions can also be invoked in the WHERE clause of a SELECT statement or DML operation:

```
SELECT  first_name, last_name, email
FROM    hr.employees
WHERE   job_id = 'IT_PROG'
AND     salary = emp_info.highest_pay('IT_PROG');

FIRST_NAME      LAST_NAME       EMAIL
--------------  -------------   --------
Bruce           Ernst           BERNST
```

Use PL/SQL tables and records in Packages

Record variables allow you to store multiple separate but related pieces of information in a single construct. Record variables can be created in three different fashions:

- Define a RECORD type and then declare a variable using that type.
- Use %TYPE to declare a record variable as a previously declared record variable type.
- Use %ROWTYPE to declare a record variable to match part or all of a row in a database table or view.

For a variable of a RECORD type, the initial value of each field is NULL unless an initial value is specified when the type is defined. For a record variable declared with %TYPE, each field inherits the initial value of its corresponding field in the referenced record. RECORD types defined in a PL/SQL block are local and are available only within the block. RECORD types defined in a package specification are public and can be referenced from outside the package when qualified with the package name. RECORD types cannot be created at the schema level. User-defined RECORD types are created by specifying a name and field definitions. Fields are defined with a name and a data type. The initial value of all fields in a record is

NULL by default. If the field is specified as NOT NULL, you must also specify a non-NULL initial value.

The package below contains five procedures. The first three demonstrate different aspect of using records or tables or both at once.

- **REC_MANUAL** – This procedure declares and defines a RECORD in the package body manually.
- **REC_ROWTYPE** – This procedure defines a RECORD in the package body using the %ROWTYPE attribute.
- **REC_ROWPART** – This procedure defines a RECORD in the package body using the %ROWTYPE attribute and a cursor to create a record composed of only part of a table row.
- **TAB** – This procedure makes use of an INDEX BY table defined in the package body.
- **TAB_OF_REC** -- This procedure combines an INDEX BY table with a RECORD.

```
CREATE PACKAGE rec_tab
AS
  PROCEDURE rec_manual;
  PROCEDURE rec_rowtype;
  PROCEDURE rec_rowpart;
  PROCEDURE tab;
  PROCEDURE tab_of_rec;

END rec_tab;


CREATE PACKAGE BODY rec_tab
AS

  -- Define a record manually
  TYPE r_emprectyp IS RECORD (
          emp_id     NUMBER,
          emp_first  VARCHAR2(30),
          emp_last   VARCHAR2(30)
          );
```

```
  r_emp_rec1    r_emprectyp;
  r_emp_rec2    r_emp_rec1%TYPE;

  -- Define a record using %ROWTYPE
  r_ctry_rec hr.countries%ROWTYPE;

  -- Define a partial row using %ROWTYPE
  CURSOR c_emp IS
    SELECT first_name, last_name, job_id
    FROM   hr.employees;
  r_emp_jobs c_emp%ROWTYPE;

  -- Define a table type
  TYPE t_region IS TABLE OF VARCHAR2(20)
    INDEX BY PLS_INTEGER;
  t_reg_tab   t_region;

  TYPE t_emps IS TABLE OF r_emprectyp
  INDEX BY PLS_INTEGER;
  t_emp_tab    t_emps;

PROCEDURE rec_manual
IS
BEGIN
  r_emp_rec1.emp_id       := 103;
  r_emp_rec1.emp_first    := 'John';
  r_emp_rec1.emp_last     := 'Jones';

  r_emp_rec2.emp_id       := 104;
  r_emp_rec2.emp_first    := 'Fred';
  r_emp_rec2.emp_last     := 'Rogers';


  DBMS_OUTPUT.PUT_LINE('Employee Record 1:');
  DBMS_OUTPUT.PUT_LINE('------------------');
  DBMS_OUTPUT.PUT_LINE('emp_id:    ' || r_emp_rec1.emp_id);
  DBMS_OUTPUT.PUT_LINE('emp_first: ' ||
r_emp_rec1.emp_first);
  DBMS_OUTPUT.PUT_LINE('emp_last:  ' || r_emp_rec1.emp_last);
  DBMS_OUTPUT.PUT_LINE(' ');
  DBMS_OUTPUT.PUT_LINE('Employee Record 2:');
  DBMS_OUTPUT.PUT_LINE('------------------');
  DBMS_OUTPUT.PUT_LINE('emp_id:    ' || r_emp_rec2.emp_id);
  DBMS_OUTPUT.PUT_LINE('emp_first: ' ||
r_emp_rec2.emp_first);
  DBMS_OUTPUT.PUT_LINE('emp_last:  ' || r_emp_rec2.emp_last);
```

```
END rec_manual;

PROCEDURE rec_rowtype
AS
BEGIN
   -- Assign values to fields:
   r_ctry_rec.country_id := 'US';
   r_ctry_rec.country_name := 'United States';
   r_ctry_rec.region_id := 2;

   -- Print fields:
   DBMS_OUTPUT.PUT_LINE('country_id:     ' ||
r_ctry_rec.country_id);
   DBMS_OUTPUT.PUT_LINE('country_name: ' ||
r_ctry_rec.country_name);
   DBMS_OUTPUT.PUT_LINE('region_id:      ' ||
r_ctry_rec.region_id);
END rec_rowtype;


PROCEDURE rec_rowpart
IS
BEGIN
   r_emp_jobs.first_name := 'Fred';
   r_emp_jobs.last_name  := 'Rogers';
   r_emp_jobs.job_id     := 'IT_PROG';

   DBMS_OUTPUT.PUT_LINE (r_emp_jobs.first_name);
   DBMS_OUTPUT.PUT_LINE (r_emp_jobs.last_name);
   DBMS_OUTPUT.PUT_LINE (r_emp_jobs.job_id);

END rec_rowpart;

PROCEDURE tab
AS
BEGIN
   t_reg_tab(1) := 'Southwest';
   t_reg_tab(2) := 'Northwest';
   t_reg_tab(3) := 'Southeast';
   t_reg_tab(4) := 'Northeast';

   FOR v_Lp IN 1..4 LOOP
      DBMS_OUTPUT.PUT_LINE('t_reg_tab(' || v_Lp || ') is: ' ||
           t_reg_tab(v_Lp));
   END LOOP;
```

```
END tab;

PROCEDURE tab_of_rec
IS
BEGIN
  r_emp_rec1.emp_id        := 103;
  r_emp_rec1.emp_first     := 'John';
  r_emp_rec1.emp_last      := 'Jones';
  t_emp_tab(1)             := r_emp_rec1;

  r_emp_rec1.emp_id        := 104;
  r_emp_rec1.emp_first     := 'Fred';
  r_emp_rec1.emp_last      := 'Rogers';
  t_emp_tab(2)             := r_emp_rec1;

  FOR v_Lp IN 1..2 LOOP
    DBMS_OUTPUT.PUT_LINE('Employee Record ' || v_Lp || ':');
    DBMS_OUTPUT.PUT_LINE('------------------');
    DBMS_OUTPUT.PUT_LINE('emp_id:    ' ||
                         t_emp_tab(v_Lp).emp_id);
    DBMS_OUTPUT.PUT_LINE('emp_first: ' ||
                         t_emp_tab(v_Lp).emp_first);
    DBMS_OUTPUT.PUT_LINE('emp_last:  ' ||
                         t_emp_tab(v_Lp).emp_last);
    DBMS_OUTPUT.PUT_LINE(' ');
  END LOOP;
END tab_of_rec;

END rec_tab;
```

The five sections below each demonstrate one of the procedures in the REC_TAB package:

REC_MANUAL

The example below calls the REC_MANUAL procedure in the REC_TAB package. The procedure makes use of the two records manually created in the package body, assigning values to them and outputting the results.

```
BEGIN
  rec_tab.rec_manual;
END;


Employee Record 1:
-----------------
emp_id:    103
emp_first: John
emp_last:  Jones

Employee Record 2:
-----------------
emp_id:    104
emp_first: Fred
emp_last:  Rogers
```

REC_ROWTYPE

The REC_ROWTYPE procedure makes use of the %ROWTYPE attribute. The %ROWTYPE attribute allows you declare a record variable that represents either a full or partial row of a database table or view. The record will contain a field for every column of the row, with the same name and data type. If the row structure of the table changes, then the structure of the record changes to match automatically.

- The record fields do not inherit the constraints of the columns. A NOT NULL column will not produce a NOT NULL field.
- The record fields do not inherit initial values of the corresponding columns. Record values will all default to NULL.

To declare a record variable against a full row of a database table or view, the syntax is: "**variable_name table_or_view_name%ROWTYPE;**". A record created in this fashion will have a field with the same name and data type of every column in the table.

The example below calls the REC_ROWTYPE procedure. This procedure uses the r_ctry_rec RECORD that has been defined in the package body using the %ROWTYPE. The procedure assigns values to the record, and then outputs the results.

```
BEGIN
   rec_tab.rec_rowtype;
END;

country_id:    US
country_name:  United States
region_id:     2
```

REC_ROWPART
It is also possible to declare a record variable against a partial row of a table or view. This is performed with the syntax: "**variable_name cursor%ROWTYPE;**" To use this syntax, you must assign a query to a cursor. A record declared against that cursor will have every column that the query selects with the corresponding data type. It is possible for the cursor to select every column in the table or only a subset. The cursor must be either an explicit cursor or a strong cursor variable. The following example defines an explicit cursor whose query selects a subset of columns from the HR.EMPLOYEES table. It then declares a record variable against the cursor:

The REC_ROWPART procedure defines a cursor against a table and then applies the %ROWTYPE attribute against it. This enables it to create a record composed of only part of a table row.

```
BEGIN
   rec_tab.rec_rowpart;
END;

Fred
Rogers
IT_PROG
```

TAB

This procedure makes use of an INDEX BY table defined in the package body as a VARCHAR variable indexed by an integer value. An index-by table is a set of key-value pairs, where each key is a unique index that acts as a locator for the associated value. The data type of the index value can be either a string type or PLS_INTEGER. Indexes are stored sorted by the index value rather than the order in which they are created. The sort order for character data types is determined by the initialization parameters NLS_SORT and NLS_COMP. Index-by tables have the following characteristics:

- Are empty (but not null) until populated.
- Can hold an unspecified number of elements, which can be accessed without knowing their positions.
- Do not need disk space or network operations.
- Cannot be manipulated via DML.

Index-by tables are intended for temporary data storage. However, they can be made persistent for the life of a database session if declared in a package specification and populated in the package body. They are appropriate for relatively small lookup tables and passing collections to and from the database server. The following example uses the TAB function to populate an index-by table and output the results::

```
BEGIN
  rec_tab.tab;
END;

t_reg_tab(1) is: Southwest
t_reg_tab(2) is: Northwest
t_reg_tab(3) is: Southeast
t_reg_tab(4) is: Northeast
```

TAB_OF_REC

This procedure makes use of an INDEX BY table defined in the package body as a RECORD variable of R_EMPRECTYP indexed by an integer value. An index-by table never has more than two 'columns': the variable being indexed and the index value. However, you can combine a record with an index-by table to tie multiple values to the same index. In this case, the table still has a variable and an index, but the record variable now contains multiple distinct values. The following example is a variant of the record example used earlier. In the initial example, two records were required to hold data for two employees. With an index-by table, a single record declaration can hold multiple individual record values. In the below example, a record type is declared to hold the individual employee values. Then an index-by table is declared to hold a table of that type. The record is populated and then assigned to the array.

```
BEGIN
   rec_tab.tab_of_rec;
END;

Employee Record 1:
-----------------
emp_id:    103
emp_first: John
emp_last:  Jones

Employee Record 2:
-----------------
emp_id:    104
emp_first: Fred
emp_last:  Rogers
```

Oracle Supplied Packages

Describe the benefits of Execute Immediate over DBMS_SQL for Native Dynamic SQL

While it is possible to run static SQL statements directly from within PL/SQL, there are limitations to what can be done in this fashion. In these cases making use of dynamic SQL is required. Dynamic SQL statements are not embedded in the PL/SQL source code. Instead, they are stored or constructed character strings that are executed as SQL by the program at runtime. The ability to dynamically change the SQL to be executed at runtime enables you to create more flexible procedures. Dynamic SQL allows you to perform tasks such as selecting from a table whose name is not known until runtime. Dynamic SQL is required in the following cases:

- SQL for which the text is unknown at compile time.
- When there is a need to perform DDL and DCL operations.
- When compilation creates schema object dependencies.

The vast majority of the cases where static SQL is not applicable can be satisfied using Native Dynamic SQL (NDS). NDS can handle most dynamic SQL statements using the EXECUTE IMMEDIATE statement. If the SQL statement is self-contained, requiring no bind variables and returning no results, then the EXECUTE IMMEDIATE statement needs no clauses. If the statement requires bind variables, each placeholder must have a corresponding bind variable in the appropriate clause of the EXECUTE IMMEDIATE statement.

For SELECT statements that return multiple rows, NDS gives you these choices:
- The EXECUTE IMMEDIATE can be used with the BULK COLLECT INTO clause.
- The OPEN FOR, FETCH, and CLOSE statements can be used in lieu of EXECUTE IMMEDIATE.

EXECUTE IMMEDIATE has these clauses:

- **INTO** -- Used to designate variables to hold the results of a SELECT statement that returns a single row
- **BULK COLLECT INTO** -- Used to designate variables to hold the results of a SELECT statement that returns multiple rows.
- **USING** -- Allows you to designate incoming or outgoing bind arguments to the dynamic SQL.

Native Dynamic SQL has the following advantages over DBMS_SQL:

- It requires much less code than to implement and is much easier to use.
- It has support for objects and collections.
- It provides better performance.

Identify the flow of execution

There are four stages to a SQL statement. Not all SQL statements will use all four.

- **Parse** -- Every SQL statement must be parsed. Parsing the statement checks the statement's syntax and associates it with the cursor (either implicit or explicit). It also verifies the existence of the objects referenced and that the correct privileges exist to process the SQL.
- **Bind** -- For SQL statements that contain input data to be supplied at runtime, placeholders in the SQL statement mark where data must be supplied. For each placeholder, values must be supplied to complete the SQL statement. When the statement is run, Oracle binds these variables to the operation. The bind step only occurs when a SQL statement contains one or more bind variables.

- **Execute** -- The server executes the statement at this point. For any SQL operation except SELECT, this is the last step.
- **Fetch** -- The fetch operation retrieves the rows that satisfy the query. The fetch operation will continue until all the rows of the query have been returned.

Use EXECUTE IMMEDIATE

The syntax for EXECUTE IMMEDIATE IS:

```
EXECUTE IMMEDIATE sql_statement
[INTO   {variable
       [,variable] ... record}]
[USING   [IN|OUT|IN OUT] bind_argument
       [, [IN|OUT|IN OUT] bind_argument] ... ];
```

The below example uses NDS to construct a SQL statement that dynamically sets the value to filter the EMPLOYEES table by **and** the column to be used. Because the EXECUTE IMMEDIATE in this example uses the INTO clause, it will fail with an error if more than one row is returned.

```
CREATE PROCEDURE get_employee(p_column   VARCHAR2,
                    p_value    VARCHAR2)
IS
  v_SQL    VARCHAR2(200);
  v_row    hr.employees%ROWTYPE;
BEGIN
  v_SQL := 'SELECT * FROM hr.employees WHERE ' ||
          p_column || ' = ''' || p_value || '''';

  EXECUTE IMMEDIATE v_SQL INTO v_row;

  DBMS_OUTPUT.PUT_LINE('Employee is ' || v_row.first_name ||
                    ' ' || v_row.last_name);
END;
```

```
BEGIN
  get_employee('employee_id', '101');
  get_employee('last_name', 'Ernst');
  get_employee('phone_number', '515.124.4369');
END;

Employee is Neena Kochhar
Employee is Bruce Ernst
Employee is Ismael Sciarra
```

Describe the use and application of some Oracle server-supplied packages

DBMS_SQL

DBMS_SQL is an Oracle supplied package that allows you to perform Data Definition Language commands (DDL) or dynamic SQL from within a PL/SQL procedure. The DBMS_SQL package is owned by the SYS schema and compiled with AUTHID CURRENT_USER. This means subprograms in the package that are called from an anonymous PL/SQL block are run using the privileges of the current user. Several of the more commonly used subprograms in the DBMS_SQL package map directly to the four stages of a SQL statement defined above:

- **PARSE** – This procedure immediately parses the SQL statement specified.
- **BIND_VARIABLE** – This procedure processes bind variables.
- **EXECUTE** – This function executes the SQL statement and returns the number of rows processed.
- **FETCH_ROWS** – This function fetches a row or rows from an open cursor.

The example below demonstrates the DBMS_SQL package being used to run a dynamic SQL statement:

```
CREATE PROCEDURE emps_ds(p_empid
hr.employees.employee_id%TYPE)
AS

  v_cursor      PLS_INTEGER;
  v_emp_first   VARCHAR2(20);
  v_emp_last    VARCHAR2(20);
  v_rows        PLS_INTEGER;
BEGIN
  v_cursor := DBMS_SQL.OPEN_CURSOR;
  DBMS_SQL.PARSE(v_cursor, 'SELECT first_name, last_name ' ||
                           'FROM   hr.employees ' ||
                           'WHERE  employee_id < :x',
DBMS_SQL.NATIVE);
  DBMS_SQL.BIND_VARIABLE(v_cursor, ':x', p_empid);
  DBMS_SQL.DEFINE_COLUMN(v_cursor, 1, v_emp_first, 20);
  DBMS_SQL.DEFINE_COLUMN(v_cursor, 2, v_emp_last, 20);
  v_rows := DBMS_SQL.EXECUTE(v_cursor);

  LOOP
    IF DBMS_SQL.FETCH_ROWS(v_cursor) = 0 then
       EXIT;
    END IF;
    DBMS_SQL.COLUMN_VALUE(v_cursor, 1, v_emp_first);
    DBMS_SQL.COLUMN_VALUE(v_cursor, 2, v_emp_last);
    DBMS_OUTPUT.PUT_LINE('Employee name: ' || v_emp_first ||
' ' ||
                                              v_emp_last);
  END LOOP;
  DBMS_SQL.CLOSE_CURSOR(v_cursor);
EXCEPTION
  WHEN OTHERS THEN
       DBMS_SQL.CLOSE_CURSOR(v_cursor);
END;

Employee name: Steven King
Employee name: Neena Kochhar
Employee name: Lex De Haan
Employee name: Alexander Hunold
```

DBMS_OUTPUT

The DBMS_OUTPUT package allows PL/SQL to display output for reporting or debugging purposes. In order for this command to display output in

SQL*Plus, you must issue the command, SET SERVEROUTPUT ON. Throughout this guide, the example code has been making use of the PUT_LINE procedure to provide visibility into what is happening in the code. While the PUT_LINE procedure is by far the most commonly used of those in the DBMS_OUTPUT package, there are other procedures. This section will provide more information on all of the procedures in the DBMS_OUTPUT package.

The various procedures in DBMS_OUTPUT are:

- **DISABLE** -- Disables calls to PUT, PUT_LINE, NEW_LINE, GET_LINE, and GET_LINES. It also purges the buffer of any remaining information. There is no need to call this procedure when using the SERVEROUTPUT option of SQL*Plus. The syntax is:

    ```
    DBMS_OUTPUT.DISABLE;
    ```

- **ENABLE** -- Enables calls to PUT, PUT_LINE, NEW_LINE, GET_LINE, and GET_LINES. If the DBMS_OUTPUT package is not activated then calls to these procedures are ignored. The syntax is:

    ```
    DBMS_OUTPUT.ENABLE (buffer_size IN INTEGER DEFAULT 20000);
    ```

- **GET_LINE** -- Retrieves a single line of buffered information. The syntax is:

    ```
    DBMS_OUTPUT.GET_LINE (line OUT VARCHAR2,
                          status OUT INTEGER);
    ```

- **GET_LINES** -- Retrieves an array of lines from the buffer. This procedure is overloaded and has two alternate calls:

    ```
    DBMS_OUTPUT.GET_LINES (lines    OUT CHARARR,
                           numlines IN OUT INTEGER);

    DBMS_OUTPUT.GET_LINES (lines    OUT DBMSOUTPUT_LINESARRAY,
                           numlines IN OUT INTEGER);
    ```

- **NEW_LINE** -- Puts an end-of-line marker. The GET_LINE Procedure and the GET_LINES Procedure return "lines" as delimited by "newlines". Every call to the PUT_LINE Procedure or NEW_LINE Procedure generates a line that is returned by GET_LINE(S). The syntax is:

  ```
  DBMS_OUTPUT.NEW_LINE;
  ```

- **PUT** -- Places a partial line in the buffer. The syntax is:

  ```
  DBMS_OUTPUT.PUT (item IN VARCHAR2);
  ```

- **PUT_LINE** -- Places a full line in the buffer (i.e. text plus a 'newline' character). The syntax is:

  ```
  DBMS_OUTPUT.PUT_LINE (item IN VARCHAR2);
  ```

The PUT Procedure and PUT_LINE Procedure in the DBMS_OUTPUT package place information in a buffer. It is possible to read information from that buffer through another trigger, procedure, or package. The buffered information can be accessed by calling the GET_LINE or and GET_LINES procedures. In this fashion, you can pass messages between different subprograms in lieu of displaying them on-screen. The example below shows this. A message is placed in the buffer in the main block and then four nested subprograms retrieve the buffered text in turn and make a change before passing it back into the buffer for the next subprogram. The message displayed at the end is the result from the PUT_LINE in the gv4 subprogram. Note that the subprograms are declared and defined in the reverse order they are called in to eliminate the need for forward declaration.

```
DECLARE
   v_msg      VARCHAR2(40);
   v_status   PLS_INTEGER;

   PROCEDURE gv4
   AS
   BEGIN
```

```
    DBMS_OUTPUT.GET_LINE(v_msg, v_status);
    v_msg := REPLACE(v_msg, ' i', ' wen');
    DBMS_OUTPUT.PUT_LINE(v_msg);
  END gv4;

  PROCEDURE gv3
  AS
  BEGIN
    DBMS_OUTPUT.GET_LINE(v_msg, v_status);
    v_msg := REPLACE(v_msg, 'ear', 'er');
    DBMS_OUTPUT.PUT_LINE(v_msg);
    gv4;
  END gv3;

  PROCEDURE gv2
  AS
  BEGIN
    DBMS_OUTPUT.GET_LINE(v_msg, v_status);
    v_msg := REPLACE(v_msg, 'apev', 'eat w');
    DBMS_OUTPUT.PUT_LINE(v_msg);
    gv3;
  END gv2;

  PROCEDURE gv1
  AS
  BEGIN
    DBMS_OUTPUT.GET_LINE(v_msg, v_status);
    v_msg := REPLACE(v_msg, 'I', 'A');
    DBMS_OUTPUT.PUT_LINE(v_msg);
    gv2;
  END gv1;
BEGIN
  DBMS_OUTPUT.PUT_LINE('I heard it through the grapevine.');
  gv1;
END;

A herd went through the great wine.
```

UTL_FILE

The UTL_FILE package provides PL/SQL programs the ability to read and write from operating system files. Its I/O capabilities are similar to standard operating system stream file I/O (OPEN, GET, PUT, CLOSE) capabilities. The files and directories that are accessible to the user through UTL_FILE are controlled by several factors. The preferred method of granting access to an operating system directory for UTL_FILE is via an Oracle directory object. Directory objects can be created for any directory accessible to the Oracle server. Read and write access on the directory objects (and therefore the OS directory) can then be granted to individual database users. In the past, accessible directories for the UTL_FILE functions were specified with the initialization parameter UTL_FILE_DIR. Granting access using this method is no longer recommended. There are a number of different procedures and functions in the UTL_FILE package. Some of the more commonly used are:

- **FCLOSE** -- Closes a file
- **FCLOSE_ALL** -- Closes all open file handles
- **FCOPY** -- Copies a contiguous portion of a file to a newly created file
- **FFLUSH** -- Physically writes all pending output to a file
- **FGETATTR** -- Reads and returns the attributes of a disk file
- **FGETPOS** -- Returns the current relative offset position within a file, in bytes
- **FOPEN** -- Opens a file for input or output
- **FREMOVE** -- Deletes a disk file, assuming that you have sufficient privileges
- **FRENAME** -- Renames an existing file to a new name.
- **GET_LINE** -- Reads text from an open file
- **GET_RAW** -- Reads a RAW string value from a file and adjusts the file pointer ahead by the number of bytes read
- **IS_OPEN** --Determines if a file handle refers to an open file
- **NEW_LINE** -- Writes one or more operating system-specific line terminators to a file
- **PUT** -- Writes a string to a file
- **PUT_LINE** -- Writes a line to a file and appends an operating system-specific line terminator

The procedure for reading and writing to files is very similar.

1. Use FOPEN to grab a handle for a file in either Read, Write, or Append mode.
2. Use GET_LINE to read, or PUT_LINE to write to the file.
3. Use FCLOSE to close the file after all lines are read/written.

Some of the named exceptions for UTL_FILE include:

- **INVALID_PATH** -- File location is invalid.
- **INVALID_MODE** -- The open_mode parameter in FOPEN is invalid.
- **INVALID_FILEHANDLE** -- File handle is invalid.
- **INVALID_OPERATION** -- File could not be opened or operated on as requested.
- **READ_ERROR** -- Destination buffer too small, or operating system error occurred during the read operation
- **WRITE_ERROR** -- Operating system error occurred during the write operation.
- **INTERNAL_ERROR** -- Unspecified PL/SQL error
- **FILE_OPEN** -- The requested operation failed because the file is open.
- **INVALID_FILENAME** -- The filename parameter is invalid.
- **ACCESS_DENIED** -- Permission to access to the file location is denied.
- **DELETE_FAILED** -- The requested file delete operation failed.
- **RENAME_FAILED** -- The requested file rename operation failed.

The example below opens a file in write mode, writes a line to it and then closes it. It then re-opens the file in read mode, pulls the line from it, and closes it again.

```
DECLARE
  v_read_data VARCHAR2(32767);
  f_fh        UTL_FILE.FILE_TYPE;
BEGIN
  f_fh := UTL_FILE.FOPEN('C_TEMP', 'utl_file.tmp', 'W');
  UTL_FILE.PUT_LINE(f_fh, 'The quick brown fox jumped over the lazy dog.');
  UTL_FILE.FCLOSE(f_fh);

  f_fh := UTL_FILE.FOPEN('C_TEMP', 'utl_file.tmp', 'R');

  UTL_FILE.GET_LINE(f_fh, v_read_data, 32767);
  UTL_FILE.FCLOSE(f_fh);

  DBMS_OUTPUT.PUT_LINE(v_read_data);
END;

The quick brown fox jumped over the lazy dog.
```

Manipulating Large Objects

Compare and contrast LONG and large object (LOB) data types

The LONG and LOB data types are both designed to store large, unstructured data, including text, graphic images, and video clips. LONG and LONG RAW are legacy data types that exist primarily for backward compatibility. Oracle has recommended the use of the newer LOB data types for the past several releases. There are numerous differences in the capabilities between the two and in the way they are stored in the database.

- The maximum size of a LONG or LONG RAW is 2 Gigabytes. LOB data types can store up to 4 Gigabytes.
- Both LONG data types only allow sequential access, but LOB data types can make use of random access.
- LOBs (except NCLOBs) can be attributes of an object type that you define.
- Only a single LONG or LONG RAW column is allowed in a given table, but multiple LOB columns are allowed.
- Data in a LONG column is stored inline with the other columns, but LOB data is stored separately from the rest of the table data.

The last point is worth elaborating one. LONG data is stored in with the other row data in tables where the column is defined. However, LOB data is stored separately. A LOB locator points to the actual LOB contents. When LOB data is queried, the locator is returned rather than the actual contents.

Describe LOB data types and how they are used

All of the LOB data types with the exception of BFILES have the following characteristics:

- They store a LOB locator, which points to the location of the LOB data.
- They participate fully in transactions, are recoverable, and can be replicated.
- Changes made by package DBMS_LOB can be committed or rolled back.
- LOB locators can span transactions (for reads only), but they cannot span sessions.

None of the LOB data types can exceed 4 Gigabytes in length. The four LOB data types are:

- **CLOB** -- The CLOB data type is used to store large blocks of character data in the database, in-line or out-of-line. It supports either fixed-width or variable-width character sets. It is interpreted by the database as a single-byte character stream.
- **NCLOB** -- The NCLOB data type is used to store large blocks of NCHAR data in the database, in-line or out-of-line. It supports either fixed-width or variable-width character sets. It is interpreted by the database as a multi-byte character stream.
- **BLOB** -- The BLOB data type is used to store large binary objects in the database, in-line or out-of-line. It is interpreted by the database as a bit stream.
- **BFILE** -- The BFILE data type is used to store large binary objects in operating system files outside the database. The BFILE variable stores a file locator that points to an operating system file on the server. The locator includes a directory alias, which specifies a full path name. BFILEs cannot be modified by Oracle. BFILEs do not participate in transactions, are not recoverable, and cannot be replicated. The maximum number of open BFILEs is set by the Oracle initialization parameter SESSION_MAX_OPEN_FILES, which is system dependent.

Oracle performs implicit conversion between CLOB and VARCHAR2 values. It cannot perform implicit conversion between other data types involving LOBS (i.e. CLOB to BLOB, BFILE to BLOB, VARCHAR2 to BLOB, etc.) There is some support for management of LOBs via SQL. However, a number of functions require the use of PL/SQL. The DBMS_LOB package provides the capability to more fully interact with LOB data types than is possible through SQL alone.

Differentiate between internal and external LOBs

Internal LOBs store data in the Oracle database itself in the datafiles of tablespaces. The internal LOB types are:

- **CLOB (character LOB)** -- Stores large amounts of text in the database character set.
- **NCLOB (national character set LOB)** -- Stores Unicode data.
- **BLOB (binary LOB)** -- Stores large amounts of binary information as a bit stream.

Internal LOBs are stored differently from other data types. When a LOB column is created, a LOB segment and a LOB index are simultaneously created. The LOB segment and LOB index are always stored in the same tablespace, but this may be a different tablespace from the one contains the rest of the table. Data in a LOB segment is stored in pieces called chunks. A chunk is a logically contiguous set of data blocks and is the smallest unit of allocation for a LOB. The row of the table where the LOB is defined stores a pointer called a LOB locator. The locator in turn points to the LOB index. When the table is queried, the LOB index is used to locate the required LOB chunks.

The only external LOB is a BFILE. When a BFILE column is added to the table, the database uses the column to store a pointer to a file in the operating system. The Oracle database can read from the operating system file but not write to it. Directory objects are used in conjunction with BFILEs to locate data. The amount of space that a BFILE consumes in the database is dependent on the length of the directory object name and the length of the file name. Because the BFILE is external to the database, it cannot make use of the same read consistency mechanism as internal LOBS. If data in the external file changes, repeated reads from the same file may produce different results.

Identify and Manage BFILEs

BFILEs are data objects stored outside the database tablespaces in operating system files. BFILEs are the only external LOB data type. Oracle provides read-only byte stream access to data stored in BFILEs. They can be accessed from any storage device accessible by your operating system, including hard disk drives, CD-ROMs, and DVDs. The database can access the data if the operating system supports stream-mode access to the files. BFILEs are typically used to hold:

- Binary data that does not change while your application is running, such as graphics.
- Data that is stored externally before being loaded into internal LOBs, where the data can then be manipulated.
- Data that is appropriate for byte-stream access, such as multimedia.
- Read-only data that is relatively large in size, to avoid taking up large amounts of room in tablespaces.

When creating a directory object or BFILEs, the following conditions must be met:

- The OS file must not be a symbolic or hard link.
- The OS directory path used by the DIRECTORY object must exist.
- The OS directory path used by the DIRECTORY object should not contain any symbolic links.

- The BFILENAME() function must be passed the directory object and filename in order to create a LOB locator that points to the external file.

The initialization parameter, SESSION_MAX_OPEN_FILES defines the maximum number of simultaneously open files in a session. The number BFILES open is counted in that total. The parameter defaults to ten. If the number of unclosed files reaches the SESSION_MAX_OPEN_FILES value, no more can be opened until one or more open files is closed. To close all open files in a session, use the DBMS_LOB.FILECLOSEALL call.

Directory Objects

In order to make use of BFILES, you must create one or more Oracle Directory objects. Oracle directories are database objects that specify an alias for a directory on the server file system. Once created, directories can be used to reference external binary file LOBs (BFILEs) and external tables files in the operating system directory aliased by them. Directory objects share a single namespace and are not owned by an individual schema.

Migrate from LONG to LOB

Oracle recommends that all new applications be created using the CLOB or NCLOB data type for large amounts of character data. If you have a legacy application with LONG columns, they can generally be changed to LOBs without requiring changes to any existing applications. SQL, PL/SQL, and OCI interfaces for LONG data can all work on LOB data as well.

The ALTER TABLE command can be used to change the underlying data type of a column from LONG to CLOB, or LONG RAW to BLOB. If any domain indexes exist on the LONG column, such as indexes for data cartridge or interMedia applications, they must be dropped first. All the constraints and triggers on the table will be preserved, but indexes must be rebuilt. An example of changing a LONG RAW to a BLOB is:

```
ALTER TABLE ocptests
MODIFY (score_report BLOB)
DISABLE STORAGE IN ROW;
```

There are several restrictions when changing LONG or LONG RAW Columns to LOBs:

- LOBs are not allowed in clustered tables.
- If a table is replicated or has materialized views, and its LONG column is changed to LOB, you might have to manually fix the replicas.
- Not all triggers are preserved when the column is changed to a LOB data type.

You can also make use of the following functions to explicitly convert data to LOB data types:
- **TO_CLOB()** – Converts CHAR, LONG, or VARCHAR2 data to CLOB.
- **TO_BLOB()** – Converts RAW or LONG RAW to BLOB.

Use the DBMS_LOB PL/SQL package

The Oracle-supplied DBMS_LOB package provides a large number of subprograms that allow you to manipulate LOB data types, including BLOBs, CLOBs, NCLOBs, BFILEs, and temporary LOBs. It can be used to access or manipulate specific parts of a LOB or complete LOBs. DBMS_LOB can read and modify BLOBs, CLOBs, and NCLOBs. It provides read-only access to BFILEs. All of the subprograms in DBMS_LOB work through LOB locators. For any of the LOB operations to succeed, a valid LOB locator must be passed to them. To work with anything other than temporary

LOBs, you must create tables with LOB columns, either internal or external, before DBMS_LOB will be able to work with them.

The DBMS_LOB package does not perform any concurrency control on rows being updated. When updating rows, you should use the SELECT FOR UPDATE or a similar mechanism to lock any rows that contain LOBs that will be updated by DBMS_LOB in order to provide for concurrency.

The DBMS_LOB package contains a number of subprograms, including the following:

Procedures

- **APPEND** -- Appends the contents of the source LOB to the destination LOB.
- **CLOSE** -- Closes a previously opened internal or external LOB.
- **COPY** -- Copies all, or part, of the source LOB to the destination LOB.
- **ERASE** -- Erases all or part of a LOB.
- **FILECLOSE** -- Closes the file.
- **FILECLOSEALL** -- Closes all previously opened files.
- **FILEGETNAME** -- Gets the directory alias and file name.
- **FILEOPEN** -- Opens a file.
- **LOADFROMFILE** -- Loads BFILE data into an internal LOB.
- **LOADBLOBFROMFILE** -- Loads BFILE data into an internal BLOB.
- **LOADCLOBFROMFILE** -- Loads BFILE data into an internal CLOB.
- **OPEN** -- Opens a LOB (internal, external, or temporary) in the indicated mode
- **READ** -- Reads data from the LOB starting at the specified offset.
- **WRITE** -- Writes data to the LOB from a specified offset.
- **WRITEAPPEND** -- Writes a buffer to the end of a LOB.

Functions

- **COMPARE** -- Compares two entire LOBs or parts of two LOBs.
- **FILEEXISTS** -- Checks if the file exists on the server.
- **FILEISOPEN** -- Checks if the file was opened using the input BFILE locators.
- **GETLENGTH** – Returns the length of the LOB.
- **INSTR** – Returns the matching position of the nth occurrence of a pattern in the LOB.
- **SUBSTR** – Returns a portion of the specified LOB.
- **ISOPEN** -- Checks to see if the LOB was already opened using the input locator.
- **ISTEMPORARY** -- Checks if the locator is pointing to a temporary LOB.

The subprograms in the DBMS_LOB package can be broken out into two types. The first type reads LOB data (COMPARE, FILEEXISTS, FILEGETNAME, FILEISOPEN, GETLENGTH, INSTR, READ, SUBSTR) and are known as observers. The second type can alter LOB values (APPEND, COPY, ERASE, FILECLOSE, FILECLOSEALL, FILEOPEN, TRIM, WRITE) and are known as mutators.

The function below uses several subprograms from the DBMS_LOB package to create a REPLACE function that works for CLOB values. It is similar to the functionality of the SQL REPLACE function:

```
CREATE FUNCTION clob_replace(p_clob      CLOB,
                             p_fromval   VARCHAR2,
                             p_toval     VARCHAR2 )
RETURN CLOB IS
  c_fromLen     CONSTANT PLS_INTEGER := LENGTH(p_fromval);
  c_toLen       CONSTANT PLS_INTEGER := LENGTH(p_toval);

  v_return      CLOB;
  v_segment     CLOB;
  v_position    PLS_INTEGER := 1 - c_toLen;
  v_offset      PLS_INTEGER := 1;
BEGIN
  IF p_fromval IS NOT NULL THEN
    WHILE v_offset < DBMS_LOB.GETLENGTH(p_clob) LOOP
      v_segment := DBMS_LOB.SUBSTR(p_clob, 32767, v_offset);
      LOOP
        v_position := DBMS_LOB.INSTR(v_segment, p_fromval,
                                     v_position + c_toLen);
        EXIT WHEN (NVL(v_position, 0) = 0)
              OR (v_position = 32767 - c_toLen);
        v_segment := TO_CLOB( DBMS_LOB.SUBSTR(v_segment,
                              v_position - 1)
                     || p_toval
                     || DBMS_LOB.SUBSTR(v_segment,
                        32767 - c_fromLen - v_position -
                        c_fromLen + 1, v_position +
                        c_fromLen));
      END LOOP;

      v_return := v_return || v_segment;
      v_offset := v_offset + 32767 - c_fromLen;
    END LOOP;
  END IF;

  RETURN(v_return);

END;
```

Create LOB columns and populate them

You can create a table with one or more LOB columns directly using SQL DDL. The DBMS_LOB package is not required. If the LOB is either a CLOB or an NCLOB, you can also populate and query it directly via SQL

```
CREATE TABLE ocp_articles (
article_id         NUMBER,
article_text       CLOB);

INSERT INTO ocp_articles
VALUES (10, 'This is a really short article');
1 rows inserted.

SELECT * FROM ocp_articles;

ARTICLE_ID ARTICLE_TEXT
---------- ------------------------------
        10 This is a really short article
```

However, while you can create a BLOB column via SQL, populating it directly with a text string generates an error. You could use the RAWTOHEX function to convert the string to hexadecimal and bypass the error but it would be pointless. BLOB columns are for storing binary data, not character data. You can also populate a BLOB column from a column that contains LONG RAW data using the Oracle-supplied TO_BLOB() subprogram.

```
CREATE TABLE ocp_articles_b (
article_id         NUMBER,
article_text       bLOB);

INSERT INTO ocp_articles_b
VALUES (10, 'This is a really short article');

Error report:
SQL Error: ORA-01465: invalid hex number
01465. 00000 -  "invalid hex number"
*Cause:
*Action:
```

You can use the UTL_FILE package to read a binary file into a PL/SQL BLOB variable and then insert that value into a BLOB column. Alternately, you can use a BFILE to point to the external file and then use the DBMS_LOB procedure LOADBLOBFROMFILE to pull the binary data in to Oracle. Since the second option is more in keeping with this topic, the example below does just that. The first section below creates a table to hold a row with a BFILE LOB locator pointing to the external file to be loaded and inserts a row pointing to an external JPG file:

```
CREATE TABLE ocp_load_target (
load_id           NUMBER,
load_file         BFILE);

INSERT INTO ocp_load_target
VALUES (10, BFILENAME('C_TEMP', 'small_image.jpg'));
1 rows inserted.


SELECT * FROM ocp_load_target;

LOAD_ID LOAD_FILE
------- ----------
     10 (BFILE)
```

The procedure below uses the DBMS_LOB package to read the binary data from the external file into a BLOB variable. The binary data in the variable is then inserted into the BLOB column created in the earlier example:

```
CREATE PROCEDURE load_ocp_articles_b (p_article_id  NUMBER)
AS
  v_bfile        BFILE :=
BFILENAME('C_TEMP','small_image.jpg');
  v_Title        VARCHAR2(100);
  v_OffSetIn     INTEGER := 1;
  v_OffSetFrom   INTEGER := 1;
  v_blob         BLOB;
BEGIN
  SELECT load_file
  INTO   v_bfile
  FROM   ocp_load_target
  WHERE  load_id = 10;

  DBMS_LOB.CREATETEMPORARY (v_blob, true);
  DBMS_LOB.OPEN(v_bfile, DBMS_LOB.LOB_READONLY);
  DBMS_LOB.OPEN(v_blob, DBMS_LOB.LOB_READWRITE);
  DBMS_LOB.LOADFROMFILE(v_blob, v_bfile, DBMS_LOB.LOBMAXSIZE,
                     v_OffSetIn, v_OffSetFrom);

  INSERT INTO ocp_articles_b
  VALUES (p_article_id, v_blob);

  DBMS_LOB.CLOSE(v_blob);
  DBMS_LOB.CLOSE(v_bfile);
END load_ocp_articles_b;


BEGIN
  load_ocp_articles_b(10);
END;

SELECT * FROM ocp_articles_b;

ARTICLE_ID ARTICLE_TEXT
---------- ---------------
        10 (BLOB)
```

Perform SQL operations on LOBS
Update LOBs with SQL

Data in CLOB columns can be updated directly and easily from SQL statements as has already been demonstrated. The previous example also showed how to use the BFILENAME function in the VALUES clause of an INSERT operation to populate a row with a LOB locator for an external file. The BFILENAME function can also be used in the SET clause of an UPDATE statement:

```
UPDATE ocp_load_target
SET    load_file = BFILENAME('C_TEMP', 'large_image.jpg')
WHERE  load_id = 10;

1 rows updated.
```

When inserting or updating rows into a table that contains CLOB or BLOB columns, the functions EMPTY_CLOB() and EMPTY_BLOB() can be used to initialize the columns to empty.

```
UPDATE ocp_articles_b
SET    article_text = EMPTY_BLOB()
WHERE  article_id = 10;

1 rows updated.
```

Just as you can INSERT values directly into CLOB columns via SQL, the UPDATE statement can be used directly. Oracle is implicitly converting the text (VARCHAR) data in the SQL statement to the CLOB data type.

```
UPDATE ocp_articles
SET    article_text = 'A change to the CLOB data'
WHERE  article_id = 10;
```

Select from LOBS

As was demonstrated earlier, CLOB data can be selected directly from a table using SQL:

```
SELECT article_id, article_text
FROM   ocp_articles;

ARTICLE_ID ARTICLE_TEXT
---------- --------------------------
        10 A change to the CLOB data
```

The SUBSTR and TRIM functions of the DBMS_LOB package can be used to display a portion of a LOB:

```
SELECT article_id, SUBSTR(article_text, 1, 10) AS TEXT_PART
FROM   ocp_articles;

ARTICLE_ID TEXT_PART
---------- ------------
        10 A change t
```

Data from a CLOB column can be selected into a VARCHAR variable in a PL/SQL block providing the variable is large enough to hold it. Oracle will implicitly convert the data type to VARCHAR2:

```
DECLARE
  v_retval    VARCHAR2(300);
BEGIN
  SELECT article_text
  INTO   v_retval
  FROM   ocp_articles
  WHERE  article_id = 10;

  DBMS_OUTPUT.PUT_LINE(v_retval);
END;

A change to the CLOB data
```

BLOB or BFILE data cannot be displayed as the result of a SELECT operation. The data cannot be implicitly converted to something that can be displayed by the environment. Depending on how the particular development tool processes the results, it may return an error if you include a BLOB or BFILE column in a SELECT or it may display some innocuous result (I.e. '(BFILE)', or '(BLOB)').

Delete LOBS

To remove the LOB locator for a row and set the content of the column to empty, use the EMPTY_CLOB() or EMPTY_BLOB() functions:

```
UPDATE ocp_articles
SET    article_text = EMPTY_CLOB()
WHERE  article_id = 10;

1 rows updated.


UPDATE ocp_articles_b
SET    article_text = EMPTY_BLOB()
WHERE  article_id = 10;

1 rows updated.
```

Rows containing LOBs can be deleted exactly as rows that do not contain LOBs.

```
DELETE FROM ocp_articles_b
WHERE  article_id = 10;

1 rows deleted.
```

Describe the use of temporary LOBs

Temporary LOBs are transient artifacts. Unlike regular LOBs, they are are not permanent and are not stored in database tables or as an operating system file. Temporary LOBs, once created, are stored in the temporary tablespace and can persist for an entire session. It is possible to specify that the temporary LOB exist only for the duration of the current program call. Temporary LOBs are used like PL/SQL variables. They allow you to perform operations on LOB data without storing the data in the database first (or possibly ever). The DBMS_LOB package contains procedures and functions that allow you to create, access, update, and free temporary LOBs.

A temporary LOB is created using the DBMS_LOB.CREATETEMPORARY() procedure:

```
DBMS_LOB.CREATETEMPORARY(lob_loc   IN OUT {BLOB | CLOB},
                        cache     IN BOOLEAN,
                        duration  IN PLS_INTEGER :=
                                     DBMS_LOB.SESSION)
```

CREATETEMPORARY will create a temporary LOB and return a LOB locator with the LOB_LOC parameter. Concurrently with the creation of the temporary LOB, a temporary LOB index will be created in the default temporary tablespace. The duration parameter allows you to specify the lifetime of the temporary LOB. It defaults to DBMS_LOB.SESSION, which means the LOB will exist until the end of the current session. If the duration parameter is set to DBMS_LOB.CALL, then the LOB will be freed at the end of the calling procedure. When a temporary LOB is created, it is already set to empty. The EMPTY_BLOB() or EMPTY_CLOB() functions are not required or allowed for temporary LOBs.

The FREETEMPORARY() procedure will free a created CLOB or BLOB in your temporary tablespace. After calling this procedure, the lob locator associated with the temporary LOB is marked invalid.

```
DBMS_LOB.FREETEMPORARY(lob_loc IN OUT NOCOPY {BLOB | CLOB})
```

The ISTEMPORARY() function can be used to determine whether or not a given lob locator is for a temporary LOB or a persistent LOB. The function returns a value of 1 for a temporary LOB and 0 for a persistent LOB.

```
DBMS_LOB.ISTEMPORARY(lob_loc IN {BLOB | CLOB})
```

The following example creates a temporary LOB. It then verifies that it is a temporary LOB, adds some text, appends some more text, and outputs the results. It then and closes the LOB and frees the space used by the temporary LOB:

```
CREATE PROCEDURE templob
AS
    v_templob     CLOB;
    v_amount      NUMBER;
    v_offset      NUMBER := 1;
    v_clobtext    VARCHAR2(100);
BEGIN
    DBMS_LOB.CREATETEMPORARY(v_templob,
                             TRUE,
                             DBMS_LOB.SESSION);

    DBMS_OUTPUT.PUT_LINE('Temp check: ' ||
         DBMS_LOB.ISTEMPORARY(v_templob));

    DBMS_LOB.OPEN(v_templob,
                  DBMS_LOB.LOB_READWRITE);


    v_clobtext := 'Text for Temp LOB testing';
    DBMS_LOB.WRITE(v_templob,
                   LENGTH(v_clobtext),
                   v_offset,
                   v_clobtext);

    v_clobtext := 'Text to append to temp LOB';
    DBMS_LOB.WRITEAPPEND(v_templob,
                         LENGTH(v_clobtext),
```

```
                    v_clobtext);

    DBMS_OUTPUT.PUT_LINE(DBMS_LOB.SUBSTR(v_templob,
DBMS_LOB.GETLENGTH(v_templob), 1));

    DBMS_LOB.CLOSE(v_templob);
    DBMS_LOB.FREETEMPORARY(v_templob);
END;


BEGIN
  templob;
END;

Temp check: 1
Text for Temp LOB testingText to append to temp LOB
```

Creating Database Triggers

Describe the different types of triggers

There are two broad classes of triggers that are based on the location where the triggers are stored:

- **Database Triggers** – Database triggers are stored in the Oracle data dictionary. They fire based on DML events, DDL events, or system events that occur in the Oracle server.
- **Application Triggers** -- Application triggers are stored (and executed) at the application level. Oracle Forms makes considerable use of application triggers for its functionality. They fire whenever a particular event occurs in the application itself.

Do not confuse application triggers with database triggers. The questions on the test will concern database triggers, although it's conceivable that a question might require that you know the difference between the two. Database triggers are broken into classes based on what triggers them:

- DML operations against a table with INSERT, UPDATE, or DELETE triggers
- DML operations against a view with an INSTEAD of trigger
- DDL statements against objects
- System Events such as startup, shutdown, or Oracle errors.

All of the above are database triggers. However, DDL and system event triggers can be set to trigger when an event occurs for a particular schema, or when it occurs for any schema in the database. Don't get confused by 'database' occurring in two different contexts when applied to triggers. The first is referring to the fact that they are stored in the dictionary and the second to the scope of the events that will trigger them.

Describe database triggers and their uses

Triggers, like subprograms, are stored in the database. However, the two are invoked in a very different fashion. Triggers can be enabled and disabled, but they not be explicitly invoked. Because they cannot be called, they are similar to anonymous PL/SQL blocks, and the documentation defines them at one point as a special kind of anonymous block. 'Named PL/SQL' is referred to in that fashion because it can be called by name. While triggers have an object name in the data dictionary, they cannot be invoked using that name, so they are not named PL/SQL.

Triggers are defined with 'triggering events' and will fire whenever that event occurs and the trigger is enabled. If disabled, it does not fire whether or not the event occurs. Triggers are defined on the items. The item may be a table, a view, a schema, or the database. The timing of when the trigger fires is also defined, and may be before or after the triggering event. There are two broad classes of database triggers:

- **DML** -- DML triggers are created on a table or view. They will have a triggering event that is composed of the DML statements DELETE, INSERT, and UPDATE. It is possible to create a MERGE trigger by creating INSERT and UPDATE triggers for statements equivalent to the MERGE operation. DML triggers are further subdivided into Simple (with a single timing point) and compound triggers (that can have multiple timing points).
- **System** -- System triggers are created either on a schema or the database. They will have a triggering event composed of either DDL or database operation statements. DDL triggering events include CREATE, ALTER, and DROP, among others, while system events include options such as STARTUP, SHUTDOWN, AND SERVERERROR.

System triggers can be defined either on the schema or the database:

- **DATABASE** -- The trigger fires whenever any database user initiates the triggering event.
- **SCHEMA** -- The trigger is created on a schema and fires whenever the user who owns it is the current user and initiates the triggering event.

Triggers can provide many different functions:
- Auditing database or modifications
- Enforcing complex data integrity rules
- Providing referential integrity
- Replicating data between locations
- Logging the occurrence of specific events
- Maintaining derived data
- Providing an additional layer of security

List guidelines for designing triggers

- Triggers should be used to guarantee that when a specific operation is performed, related actions are performed.
- Triggers should not duplicate features already built into Oracle.
- The body of triggers should be relatively small. When trigger bodies exceed 50-60 lines, the code should be placed in a stored procedure and called from the trigger.
- Triggers should be used for centralized, global operations that should be fired for the triggering statement, regardless of which user or application it.
- Triggers should never be recursive. When one trigger issues a statement that fires a trigger, it can cause recursive firing until it has run out of memory.
- DATABASE triggers should be used sparingly. They are executed for every user every time the event occurs on which the trigger is created.

Create a DML trigger

The example below creates a simple BEFORE INSERT trigger against the HR.EMPLOYEES table. Whenever a row is inserted into the table, it outputs the first and last name of the employee being inserted and their job ID.

```
CREATE OR REPLACE TRIGGER hr.tr_employee_insert
  BEFORE INSERT
  ON hr.employees
  FOR EACH ROW
BEGIN
    DBMS_OUTPUT.PUT_LINE('Inserting ' || :NEW.first_name ||
          ' ' || :NEW.last_name || ' -- ' || :NEW.job_id ||
          ' into employees');
END tr_employee_insert;
```

The trigger cannot be called directly like a stored procedure. To test it requires inserting a row into the table. The example below inserts a partial row into the table:

```
INSERT INTO hr.employees (employee_id, first_name, last_name,
                          job_id, email)
VALUES (300, 'John', 'Doe', 'IT_PROG', 'jdoe@company.com');

Inserting John Doe -- IT_PROG into employees

Error report:
SQL Error: ORA-01400: cannot insert NULL into
("HR"."EMPLOYEES"."HIRE_DATE")
01400. 00000 -  "cannot insert NULL into (%s)"
*Cause:
*Action:
```

The INSERT failed with an ORA-1400 error, but the trigger still fired. This happened because a BEFORE INSERT trigger fires before the INSERT is attempted. One real-life use of a BEFORE INSERT trigger would be to check for problems like the above such as required column values missing from the INSERT statement to prevent an unhandled exception. In the below example, the trigger timing is changed to AFTER INSERT and the operation is attempted again:

```
CREATE OR REPLACE TRIGGER hr.tr_employee_insert
  AFTER INSERT
  ON hr.employees
  FOR EACH ROW
BEGIN
   DBMS_OUTPUT.PUT_LINE('Inserting ' || :NEW.first_name ||
                       ' ' || :NEW.last_name || ' -- ' ||
                       :NEW.job_id || ' into employees');
END tr_employee_insert;

INSERT INTO hr.employees (employee_id, first_name, last_name, job_id, email)
VALUES (300, 'John', 'Doe', 'IT_PROG', 'jdoe@company.com');

Error report:
SQL Error: ORA-01400: cannot insert NULL into
("HR"."EMPLOYEES"."HIRE_DATE")
01400. 00000 -  "cannot insert NULL into (%s)"
*Cause:
*Action:
```

This time we still get the ORA-1400 error, but the trigger did not fire. AFTER INSERT triggers are used to perform some action after a successful INSERT. If the INSERT does not happen, the trigger will not fire. The same success/fail logic applies to the timing of UPDATE and DELETE triggers as well, of course. If the outcome of a trigger might be to block the DML operation being performed, it is more efficient for it to be a BEFORE rather than an AFTER trigger. If the trigger causes the operation to fail with AFTER timing, the database must make the changes and then roll them back. It would be faster to prevent the operation from ever occurring.

List the DML trigger components

The CREATE TRIGGER statement creates or replaces a database trigger, which can be either of these:

- A stored PL/SQL block associated with a table, a schema, or the database
- An anonymous PL/SQL block or an invocation of a procedure implemented in PL/SQL or Java

When the conditions specified in the trigger occur, the trigger is fired automatically. The CREATE TRIGGER statement has a large number of optional components to it. These are necessary to provide the ability to define the specific conditions required for the trigger to be fired. The body of a trigger can contain DML SQL statements. Triggers may contain SELECT statements, but they must be SELECT... INTO... statements or the SELECT statement in the definition of a cursor. DDL and transaction control statements are not allowed in the body of a trigger. System triggers can issue {CREATE/ALTER/DROP} TABLE statements and ALTER...COMPILE operations. The basic syntax to create a trigger is:

```
CREATE TRIGGER trigger_name
BEFORE | AFTER | INSTEAD OF
trigger_event1 [OR trigger_event2 OR trigger_event3]
ON object_name
[REFERENCING OLD AS old / NEW as new]
[FOR EACH ROW]
[WHEN (condition)]
BEGIN
   trigger_body
[EXCEPTION]
END [trigger_name];

trigger_event = INSERT | UPDATE [OF column_list] | DELETE
```

- A DML trigger can only be created on a single table.
- If a database trigger fails, the DML operation that invoked the trigger is rolled back.

- Database triggers are implicitly executed by the triggering event. To execute a trigger, you must perform one of these events.

Describe the trigger firing sequence options

A DML trigger fires at only one of four timing points:

- Before the triggering statement runs
- After the triggering statement runs
- Before each row that the triggering statement affects
- After each row that the triggering statement affects

When DML triggers fire at the row level, they can access the data in the row being processed. With the exception of INSTEAD OF triggers, triggers fired on an UPDATE can include a column list. When a column list is provided, the trigger fires only when one or more of the specified columns are updated. When no column list is provided, the trigger fires when any column in the table is updated.

Trigger timing is specified using the BEFORE or AFTER keywords. If the trigger body should execute before the event, use BEFORE. If the trigger body should execute after the event, use AFTER. Trigger events include INSERT, UPDATE, and DELETE. If the event is for an UPDATE of any column in the triggering table, use UPDATE ON <table name>. If the event is an update of a particular column or columns, use UPDATE OF <column name, column name> ON <table_name>.

For example:

```
AFTER UPDATE ON hr.employees

AFTER UPDATE OF salary ON hr.employees
```

Use conditional predicates in a DML trigger

The triggering event of DML triggers can be composed of more than one triggering statements. Conditional predicates allow the trigger to determine which statement was the source of the current execution. The predicates are referenced as a BOOLEAN expression. The conditional predicates are:

- **INSERTING** -- An INSERT statement fired the trigger.
- **UPDATING** -- An UPDATE statement fired the trigger.
- **UPDATING ('column')** -- An UPDATE statement that affected the specified column fired the trigger.
- **DELETING** -- A DELETE statement fired the trigger.

The below example creates a BEFORE statement trigger named TR_EMPLOYEE_TEST with multiple triggering events for the table HR.EMPLOYEES. It fires whenever there is an INSERT, an UPDATE of the JOB_ID field, or on a DELETE. After creating the trigger, an UPDATE and DELETE operation against the table demonstrate that the trigger fired as expected and that the UPDATING and DELETING predicates functioned properly.

```
CREATE OR REPLACE TRIGGER hr.tr_employee_test
  BEFORE
    INSERT OR
    UPDATE OF job_id OR
    DELETE
  ON hr.employees
  FOR EACH ROW
BEGIN
  CASE
    WHEN INSERTING THEN
      DBMS_OUTPUT.PUT_LINE('Row inserted into employees');
    WHEN UPDATING('JOB_ID') THEN
      DBMS_OUTPUT.PUT_LINE('Updating ' || :OLD.job_id || ' to ' ||
          :NEW.job_id || ' for employee #: ' ||
:OLD.employee_id);
    WHEN DELETING THEN
```

```
      DBMS_OUTPUT.PUT_LINE('Deleting employee #: ' ||
:OLD.employee_id);
  END CASE;
END tr_employee_test;


UPDATE hr.employees
SET    job_id = 'IT_PROG'
WHERE employee_id = 102;

Updating AD_VP to IT_PROG for employee #: 102

DELETE FROM hr.employees
WHERE   email = 'KCOLMENA';

Deleting employee #: 119
```

Create a row level trigger

Row-level triggers fire one time for each row affected by a statement (if no rows are affected, they will not fire). They are created using the FOR EACH ROW clause in the CREATE TRIGGER statement. This example creates a BEFORE row trigger with a condition. It will only fire when the JOB_ID field is being updated to AD_VP.

```
CREATE OR REPLACE TRIGGER hr.tr_employee_test
  BEFORE
    UPDATE OF job_id
  ON hr.employees
  FOR EACH ROW
    WHEN (NEW.job_id = 'AD_VP')
BEGIN
  DBMS_OUTPUT.PUT_LINE('Too many chiefs. Not enough
indians.');
END tr_employee_test;

UPDATE hr.employees
SET    job_id = 'AD_VP'
WHERE employee_id = 120;

Too many chiefs. Not enough indians.
```

Create a statement level trigger

Statement-level triggers fire one time when the triggering statement is executed. They will fire one time even if no rows are affected by the triggering statement. They are the default option when creating a trigger. Statement-level triggers cannot access the :NEW or :OLD pseudorecords as row-level triggers can. The example below creates an AFTER UPDATE trigger that outputs the database user, date and time when the HR.EMPLOYEES table is updated.

```
CREATE OR REPLACE TRIGGER hr.tr_employee_test
  AFTER UPDATE ON hr.employees
BEGIN
  DBMS_OUTPUT.PUT_LINE(USER || ' has just updated the HR.EMPLOYEES table at ' ||
    TO_CHAR(SYSDATE, 'DD-MON-YYYY HH24:MI'));
END tr_employee_test;

UPDATE hr.employees
SET    phone_number = '590.423.4586'
WHERE  employee_id = 104;

OCPGURU has just updated the HR.EMPLOYEES table at 14-JUL-2012 23:54
```

Use the OLD and NEW qualifiers in a database trigger

Row-level triggers have the ability to access data that is in the row being changed through the use of correlation names. By default, triggers use the correlation names OLD and NEW. The REFERENCING clause of the CREATE TRIGGER statement allows you to alter the correlation names. The OLD and NEW values are also known as pseudorecords. The structure of a pseudorecord is table_name%ROWTYPE, where table_name is the name of the table on which the trigger is created. In the trigger body, a correlation name is a placeholder for a bind variable. The field of a pseudorecord can be referenced using the following syntax:

```
:pseudorecord_name.field_name    (i.e. :NEW.employee_id)
```

If a pseudorecord is used in the WHEN clause of a conditional trigger, the correlation name is not a placeholder for a bind variable. The pseudorecord field is referenced without a colon prefix.

```
pseudorecord_name.field_name    (i.e. NEW.employee_id)
```

The values contained by the pseudorecords for the three DML operations are:

- **INSERT** -- The OLD field contains NULL and the NEW field contains the post-insert value.
- **UPDATE** -- The OLD field contains the pre-update value and the NEW field contains the post-update value.
- **DELETE** -- The OLD field contains the pre-delete value and the NEW field contains NULL.

There are several restrictions on pseudorecords:

- A pseudorecord cannot appear in a record-level operation. (e.g. :NEW := NULL; is illegal)
- A pseudorecord cannot be an actual subprogram parameter, but a pseudorecord field can be (i.e. :NEW cannot be a parameter but :NEW.employee_id can be).
- The trigger cannot change OLD field values.
- The trigger cannot change NEW field values on a DELETE trigger.
- An AFTER trigger cannot change NEW field values.

BEFORE triggers can change NEW field values before the triggering INSERT or UPDATE statement puts them in the table. If the same DML statement also has an AFTER trigger, then the AFTER trigger will see the changed values put in place by the BEFORE trigger. The example below creates a table to audit salary changes in the HR.EMPLOYYES table. Whenever the salary column is updated, the old and new values are records, along with the employee ID, date changes, and schema making the change:

```
CREATE TABLE emp_audit_salary (
employee_id    NUMBER,
change_date    DATE,
old_salary     NUMBER,
new_salary     NUMBER,
changed_by     VARCHAR2(32)
);

CREATE OR REPLACE TRIGGER tr_emp_audit_salary
AFTER UPDATE OF salary ON hr.employees
FOR EACH ROW
BEGIN
  INSERT INTO emp_audit_salary
  VALUES (:NEW.employee_id, SYSDATE, :OLD.salary,
       :NEW.salary, USER);
END tr_emp_audit_salary;

UPDATE hr.employees
SET    salary = 13000
WHERE  employee_id = 108;

SELECT *
FROM   emp_audit_salary;

EMPLOYEE_ID CHANGE_DATE OLD_SALARY NEW_SALARY CHANGED_BY
----------- ----------- ---------- ---------- -----------
        108 15-JUL-12        12008      13000 OCPGURU
```

Create an INSTEAD OF trigger

INSTEAD OF triggers are a type of DML trigger created against a view that cannot be updated normally (a noneditioning view), or on a nested table column of a noneditioning view. When a DML statement is issued against the view, the database fires the INSTEAD OF trigger "instead of" performing the DML operation. It is not possible for INSTEAD OF triggers to be conditional. These triggers provide the only means of updating views that cannot be updated directly via DML. The trigger must be designed to determine the intended operation and to perform the equivalent operations on the underlying table(s). INSTEAD OF triggers are always row-level rather than statement-level. They can read the OLD and NEW values, but cannot alter them.

INSTEAD OF triggers provide a transparent way of modifying views that are not inherently modifiable directly through DML statements. BEFORE and AFTER triggers execute before and after triggering DML events. If a view does not allow DML, these trigger types will not fire. An INSTEAD OF trigger must be used. The example below shows how you can use an INSTEAD OF trigger in order to perform DML on a view that would otherwise not be possible. The view EMPLOYEES_DEPT_V is created:

```
CREATE OR REPLACE VIEW employees_dept_v AS
  SELECT employee_id, last_name, hire_date, email,
         job_id, d.department_id, department_name
    FROM hr.employees e
         INNER JOIN hr.departments d
         ON e.department_id = d.department_id;
```

Normally this view would not be updatable, because the primary key of the HR.DEPARTMENTS is not unique in the result set of the join view. An attempt to INSERT into the table produces an ORA-1779 error:

```
INSERT INTO employees_dept_v
VALUES (310, 'Doe', '10-JAN-12', 'JDOE', 'IT_PROG',
        30, 'Human Resources');

Error report:
SQL Error: ORA-01779: cannot modify a column which maps to a
non key-preserved table
01779. 00000 -  "cannot modify a column which maps to a non
key-preserved table"
*Cause:    An attempt was made to insert or update columns of
a join view which
           map to a non-key-preserved table.
*Action:   Modify the underlying base tables directly.
```

It is possible to make this view updatable by creating an INSTEAD OF trigger against the view. The trigger will fire when in INSERT is issued against the view and the actions in the trigger will be performed instead of Oracle attempting to process in INSERT statement directed against the view.

```
CREATE TRIGGER tr_insert_emp_dept_v
   INSTEAD OF INSERT ON employees_dept_v
DECLARE
  v_count     NUMBER;
BEGIN
  SELECT COUNT(*)
  INTO   v_count
  FROM   hr.departments
  WHERE  department_id = :NEW.department_id
  AND    department_name = :NEW.department_name;

  IF v_count = 1 THEN
    -- Department already exists.
    -- Just insert employee record.
    INSERT INTO hr.employees (employee_id, last_name,
                              hire_date, email, job_id,
                              department_id)
    VALUES (:NEW.employee_id, :NEW.last_name, :NEW.hire_date,
            :NEW.email, :NEW.job_id, :NEW.department_id);
  ELSE
    SELECT COUNT(*)
    INTO   v_count
    FROM   hr.departments
    WHERE  department_id = :NEW.department_id;

    IF v_count = 0 THEN
      -- New Department. Insert employee record
      -- and department record.
      INSERT INTO hr.employees (employee_id, last_name,
                                hire_date, email, job_id,
                                department_id)
      VALUES (:NEW.employee_id, :NEW.last_name,
              :NEW.hire_date, :NEW.email, :NEW.job_id,
              :NEW.department_id);

      INSERT INTO hr.departments (department_id,
                                  department_name)
      VALUES (:NEW.department_id, :NEW.department_name);
    ELSE
      DBMS_OUTPUT.PUT_LINE('Department ID exists, but name does not match');
    END IF;
```

```
  END IF;
END tr_insert_emp_dept_v;
```

Once this trigger is in place, the INSERT against the view now succeeds:

```
INSERT INTO employees_dept_v
VALUES (310, 'Doe', '10-JAN-12', 'JDOE', 'IT_PROG',
        30, 'Purchasing');

SELECT last_name, hire_date, email, job_id,
       Department_name
FROM   employees_dept_v
WHERE  employee_id = 105;

LAST_NAME  HIRE_DATE  EMAIL    JOB_ID    DEPARTMENT_NAME
---------  ---------  -------  --------  ---------------
Doe        10-JAN-12  JDOE     IT_PROG   Purchasing
```

Describe the difference between stored procedures and triggers

Stored Procedures -- A stored procedure is a named PL/SQL block that is stored in the data dictionary. Because they are named and available in the dictionary tables, named blocks can be invoked repeatedly. Stored procedure can contain parameters, and the values of these can be different for each invocation.

- Can accept parameters while a trigger cannot.
- Can return values to the invoking process.
- Can be (and must be) explicitly called.
- Is not associated with any particular database object.

Triggers -- A trigger is a special kind of PL/SQL anonymous block that can be defined to fire before or after SQL statements or for certain system events. When triggered by a DML operation, they can fire either on a statement level or for each row that is affected. It is also possible to define INSTEAD OF triggers or system triggers. Triggers are stored in the data dictionary and can be reused repeatedly, but cannot be explicitly invoked. Triggers are invoked automatically by certain database events.

- Cannot accept parameters.
- Cannot return any value.
- Executed automatically on some event.
- Can call a stored procedure (but the reverse is not possible).
- DML triggers are associated with a specific object (table/view).

Describe the trigger execution model

Triggers always execute as the definer of the trigger. The trigger action of an event is always executed as the definer of the action. This is the definer of the package or function in callouts, or the owner of the trigger in queues. The owner of the trigger must have EXECUTE privileges on the underlying queues, packages, or procedure.

Essentially this means that the schema which creates the event that fires the trigger does not even need to have the privileges to perform the functions performed in the trigger body.

Alter a trigger status

The CREATE TRIGGER statement will create a trigger as enabled by default. It is possible to create a trigger in the disabled state by using the DISABLE keyword. Triggers that are created in the disabled state can be tested for compile-time errors before they are enabled. In addition, you might want to temporarily disable triggers for several reasons:

- The object the trigger refers to is temporarily unavailable.
- There is going to be a large data load against the table that you would like to have run without firing triggers.
- The existing data in the table is being reloaded and the trigger would make unwanted changes (i.e. a trigger that generates a primary key using a sequence).

A single trigger can be enabled or disabled using the ALTER TRIGGER statement:

```
ALTER TRIGGER [schema.]trigger_name { ENABLE | DISABLE };
```

All of the triggers on a single table can be enabled or disabled using the ALTER TABLE statement:

```
ALTER TABLE [schema].table_name { ENABLE | DISABLE } ALL TRIGGERS;
```

The schema in both statements must be the name of the schema containing the trigger. If not supplied, it will default to the current schema

An invalid trigger can be recompiled using the ALTER TRIGGER statement:

```
ALTER TRIGGER trigger_name COMPILE;
```

It is not possible to change the code of a trigger using the ALTER TRIGGER statement. ALTER TRIGGER only allows you to enable, disable, compile, or rename a trigger. You can replace a trigger using the CREATE TRIGGER statement with the OR REPLACE clause. Alternately, you can re-create a trigger by dropping it with the DROP TRIGGER statement and then creating it with the CREATE TRIGGER statement.

Remove a trigger

To remove unwanted triggers, you use the DROP TRIGGER statement:

```
DROP TRIGGER trigger_name;
```

The DROP command is a DDL operation and will implicitly commit.

More Trigger Concepts

Define what a database trigger is
Database triggers can be divided into those for DML events, system and client events.

- **DML events** – DML events include Data Manipulation Language operations that alter data (SELECT is sometimes considered a black-sheep DML. There is no trigger for it).

- **System events** – These events related to entire instances or schemas, not individual tables or rows. System events are particular database states that can be used to fire a system trigger. Triggers created on startup and shutdown events must be associated with the database instance. Triggers created on error and suspend events can be associated with either the database instance or a particular schema. When a triggering event occurs, the database will open an autonomous transaction scope, fire the trigger, and commit any transaction imbedded in the trigger. For schema-level triggers, this will not affect any existing user transaction in the triggering session.

- **Client events** -- These events are related to user logon/logoff, DCL, and DDL operations.

Describe events that cause database triggers to fire
DML Events are:

- **INSERT** – An INSERT operation on a table.
- **UPDATE** – An UPDATE operation on a table.
- **DELETE** – A DELETE operation on a table.

Some examples of system events are:

- **AFTER STARTUP** -- Causes the database to fire the trigger whenever the database is opened. This event is valid only with DATABASE, not with SCHEMA.
- **BEFORE SHUTDOWN** -- Causes the database to fire the trigger whenever an instance of the database is shut down. This event is valid only with DATABASE, not with SCHEMA.
- **AFTER SERVERERROR** -- Causes the database to fire the trigger whenever a server error message is logged. There are a handful of database errors that will not raise this event. See the PL/SQL Language Reference for details.

Some examples of client events are:

- **BEFORE/AFTER ALTER** -- When a catalog object is altered.
- **BEFORE/AFTER DROP** -- When a catalog object is dropped.
- **BEFORE/AFTER ANALYZE** -- When an analyze statement is issued
- **BEFORE/AFTER AUDIT** -- When an audit statement is issued
- **BEFORE/AFTER NOAUDIT** -- When a noaudit statement is issued
- **BEFORE/AFTER COMMENT** -- When an object is commented.
- **BEFORE/AFTER CREATE**-- When a catalog object is created.
- **BEFORE/AFTER DDL** -- When most SQL DDL statements are issued.
- **BEFORE/AFTER GRANT**-- When a grant statement is issued.
- **BEFORE LOGOFF** -- At the start of a user logoff.
- **AFTER LOGON** -- After a successful logon of a user.
- **BEFORE/AFTER RENAME** -- When a rename statement is issued.

Create a trigger for a DDL statement

DDL triggers are created as system triggers for client events and therefore must be created either at the schema or database level. When created at the schema level, the trigger will fire whenever the user that owns the trigger initiates the triggering event. If any other user performs that event, the trigger will not fire. By contrast, a database-level trigger will fire whenever any user initiates the event. The example below creates a trigger against the PLEASE_CHANGEME table in the HR schema. The user OCPGURU then issues an ALTER TABLE statement against the table and the trigger does not fire.

```
CREATE TABLE please_changeme (
col1    NUMBER);

CREATE OR REPLACE TRIGGER tr_hr_noalter
BEFORE ALTER ON hr.SCHEMA
BEGIN
  RAISE_APPLICATION_ERROR (
    num => -20001,
    msg => 'HR Cannot alter objects');
END;

ALTER TABLE please_changeme ADD (col2 NUMBER);
table PLEASE_CHANGEME altered.
```

In the below example, the previous schema-level trigger is dropped and a new one created on the OCPGURU schema. The alter table statement is attempted again and this time fails with the supplied error.

```
DROP TRIGGER tr_hr_noalter;
CREATE OR REPLACE TRIGGER tr_ocpguru_noalter
BEFORE ALTER ON ocpguru.SCHEMA
BEGIN
  RAISE_APPLICATION_ERROR (
    num => -20001,
    msg => 'OCPGuru Cannot alter objects');
END;

ALTER TABLE please_changeme ADD (col3 NUMBER);
ORA-20001: OCPGuru Cannot alter objects
```

Create a trigger for a system event

The example below makes use of the AFTER SERVERERROR to fire a trigger when an ORA-1722 error is raised:

```
CREATE OR REPLACE TRIGGER tr_nota_number
AFTER SERVERERROR ON DATABASE
BEGIN
  IF (IS_SERVERERROR (1722)) THEN
    DBMS_OUTPUT.PUT_LINE('Someone doesn''t know what a number is again');
  END IF;
END;

INSERT INTO hr.departments
VALUES (400, 'New Department', 'A14', '5345');

Error report:
SQL Error: ORA-01722: invalid number

Someone doesn't know what a number is again
```

Describe the functionality of the CALL statement

It's also possible to have a trigger invoke a subprogram using the CALL clause. Subprograms invoked using CALL can be implemented in PL/SQL, C, or Java. The CALL functionality is useful if two or more different database triggers perform the exact same code. You can create a procedure with the required code (parameterized if necessary) and have each database trigger execute the new procedure. This reduces redundant code and means any future modifications to the code only occur in one location. The below example creates a procedure called JOB_CHANGE that accepts the old and new JOB_ID values. The TR_EMPLOYEES_TEST trigger is then created to call the new function:

```
CREATE PROCEDURE hr.job_change(p_old_job    VARCHAR2,
                               p_new_job    VARCHAR2)
AS
BEGIN
  IF p_old_job = 'IT_PROG' AND
     p_new_job = 'AD_VP' THEN
     DBMS_OUTPUT.PUT_LINE('What kind of programmer becomes a
VP voluntarily?');
  ELSE
     DBMS_OUTPUT.PUT_LINE('Too many chiefs. Not enough
indians.');
  END IF;
END job_change;


CREATE OR REPLACE TRIGGER hr.tr_employee_test
  BEFORE
     UPDATE OF job_id
  ON hr.employees
  FOR EACH ROW
     WHEN (NEW.job_id = 'AD_VP')
CALL job_change(:OLD.job_id, :NEW.job_id)

UPDATE hr.employees
SET    job_id='AD_VP'
WHERE  employee_id = 103;

What kind of programmer becomes a VP voluntarily?
```

Describe the cause of a mutating table

When a table is currently being modified by a DML statement, it is considered to be mutating. Oracle has a mutating-table restriction that is intended to prevent triggers from querying or modifying the table that the triggering statement is simultaneously modifying. Oracle cannot guarantee read-consistency when a table is mutating. If a row-level trigger tries to query or update a mutating table, an ORA-04091 error will be returned. Any changes made by the trigger and the triggering statement will be rolled back, and control returned to the user or application. The example below demonstrates the mutating table error. A DELETE trigger is added to the employees table. In the trigger body, a SELECT statement counts the number of rows currently in the table and outputs them. However, because the table is changing (one or more rows are being removed), it is mutating and so the SELECT statement that is attempting to count the rows generates the ORA-4091 error:

```
CREATE OR REPLACE TRIGGER tr_count_on_delete
AFTER DELETE ON hr.employees
FOR EACH ROW
DECLARE
  v_employees PLS_INTEGER;
BEGIN
  SELECT COUNT(*)
  INTO   v_employees
  FROM   hr.employees;
  DBMS_OUTPUT.PUT_LINE('At the sound of the bell, there will be ' ||
                       v_employees || ' employees.');
END tr_count_on_delete;


DELETE FROM hr.employees
WHERE  employee_id = 110;

Error report:
SQL Error: ORA-04091: table HR.EMPLOYEES is mutating, trigger/function may not see it
ORA-06512: at "OCPGURU.TR_COUNT_ON_DELETE", line 4
ORA-04088: error during execution of trigger 'OCPGURU.TR_COUNT_ON_DELETE'
04091. 00000 -  "table %s.%s is mutating, trigger/function may not see it"
*Cause:    A trigger (or a user defined plsql function that
           is referenced in this statement) attempted to look
           at (or modify) a table that was in the middle of
           being modified by the statement which fired it.
*Action:   Rewrite the trigger (or function) so it does not
           read that table.
```

Note that the same trigger created as a statement level AFTER DELETE does not generate the ORA-4091. In this case, the DELETE operation has completed and so there is no mutation happening at the time the SELECT statement tries to count the employees:

```
CREATE OR REPLACE TRIGGER tr_count_on_delete
AFTER DELETE ON hr.employees
DECLARE
  v_employees PLS_INTEGER;
BEGIN
  SELECT COUNT(*)
  INTO    v_employees
  FROM    hr.employees;
  DBMS_OUTPUT.PUT_LINE('At the sound of the bell, ' ||
      'there will be ' || v_employees || ' employees.');
END tr_count_on_delete;

DELETE FROM hr.employees
WHERE   employee_id = 110;

At the sound of the bell, there will be 107 employees.
```

It is worth noting that mutating table issues are not just related to triggers. The example below demonstrates a mutating table condition using the HIGHEST_PAY function of the EMP_INFO package. The function returns the highest pay for a given job ID. However, when that function is used in an UPDATE statement that is altering the salary, an ORA-4091 error is returned. Because the UPDATE operation is changing the salary, it is not possible to simultaneously determine the highest salary.

```
FUNCTION highest_pay(p_job_id    hr.employees.job_id%TYPE)
RETURN NUMBER
AS
   v_retval    NUMBER;

BEGIN
   SELECT MAX(salary)
   INTO    v_retval
   FROM    hr.employees
   WHERE   job_id = p_job_id;

   RETURN v_retval;

END highest_pay;
```

```
UPDATE hr.employees
SET    salary = salary * .95
WHERE  job_id = 'AD_VP'
AND    salary = emp_info.highest_pay('AD_VP');

Error report:
SQL Error: ORA-04091: table HR.EMPLOYEES is mutating,
trigger/function may not see it
ORA-06512: at "OCPGURU.EMP_INFO", line 10
04091. 00000 -  "table %s.%s is mutating, trigger/function
may not see it"
*Cause:    A trigger (or a user defined plsql function that
           is referenced in this statement) attempted to look
           at (or modify) a table that was in the middle of
           being modified by the statement which fired it.
*Action:   Rewrite the trigger (or function) so it does not
           read that table.
```

List what triggers can be implemented for

Triggers can perform a broad range of functions in a database. The ability to create code that executes automatically based on certain events allows developers to make a database more responsive. Some of the common uses for database triggers are:

- Populate primary key values automatically.
- Generate virtual column values.
- Generate log entries for events.
- Generate table access statistics.
- Modify table data when DML statements are issued against views
- Replicate data changes in local tables to tables in a remote database
- Enforce referential integrity when related tables are on different nodes of a distributed database
- Publish information about database events, user events, and SQL statements to subscribing applications
- Restrict DML operations on tables to regular business hours
- Prevent invalid transactions

- Enforce complex business or referential integrity rules that aren't possible with constraints
- Maintaining the values of columns that are derived from data in another table.

List the privileges associated with triggers

- **CREATE TRIGGER** -- Allows you to create a trigger on tables in your schema. You must also either own the specified in the triggering statement, or have the ALTER privilege for the table in the triggering statement, or the ALTER ANY TABLE system privilege.
- **CREATE ANY TRIGGER** -- Allows you to create a trigger in another user's schema, or to reference a table in another schema from a trigger in your schema.
- **ADMINISTER DATABASE TRIGGER** -- Allows you to create a trigger on DATABASE. If this privilege is later revoked, you can drop any existing triggers, but not alter them.

If any procedures, functions, or packages are referenced from the trigger, the user must have EXECUTE access on them. The object privileges for any schema objects referenced in the trigger body must be granted to the trigger's owner explicitly (not through a role). The statements in the trigger body operate under the privilege domain of the trigger's owner, rather than the user issuing the triggering statement.

View trigger information in the dictionary views

You can view information about triggers using the USER_TRIGGERS view (or the ALL_TRIGGERS or DBA_TRIGGERS views). The source of a database trigger can be found in the TRIGGER_BODY column. The status of the trigger (ENABLED or DISABLED) can be found in the STATUS column. The

USER_OBJECTS view also has a STATUS column which can be used to determine whether a trigger is valid or invalid. The following example demonstrates pulling the trigger body from USER_TRIGGERS:

```
SELECT trigger_body
FROM   all_triggers
WHERE  trigger_name = 'TR_EMPLOYEE_TEST';

TRIGGER_BODY
---------------------------------------------------------------
BEGIN
  CASE
    WHEN INSERTING THEN
      DBMS_OUTPUT.PUT_LINE('Row inserted into employees');
    WHEN UPDATING('JOB_ID') THEN
      DBMS_OUTPUT.PUT_LINE('Updating ' || :OLD.job_id ||
         ' to ' || :NEW.job_id || ' for employee #: ' ||
         :OLD.employee_id);
    WHEN DELETING THEN
      DBMS_OUTPUT.PUT_LINE('Deleting employee #: ' ||
                          :OLD.employee_id);
  END CASE;
END tr_employee_test;


SELECT trigger_type, triggering_event, table_owner, status
FROM   all_triggers
WHERE  trigger_name = 'TR_EMPLOYEE_TEST';

TRIGGER_TYPE       TRIGGERING_EVENT   TABLE_OWNER    STATUS
----------------   ----------------   ------------   --------
AFTER STATEMENT    UPDATE             HR             ENABLED



SELECT object_type, created, last_ddl_time, status
FROM   all_objects
WHERE  object_name = 'TR_EMPLOYEE_TEST';

OBJECT_TYPE           CREATED    LAST_DDL_TIME  STATUS
------------------    ---------  -------------  -------
TRIGGER               30-JUN-12  14-JUL-12      VALID
```

Managing Dependencies

Track procedural dependencies

Procedures and functions sometimes have dependencies on other objects. If stored subprograms include SQL statements against tables or views, invoke other stored subprograms, or generate values from a sequence, then they are said to reference those objects. If, for example, the code of a given subprogram includes a reference to a table in the database, then the subprogram is a dependent object of the table and the table is a referenced object of the procedure.

Dependencies for subprograms can be either direct or indirect. Direct dependencies are for objects directly referenced by the subprogram. Indirect dependencies are when an object directly referenced by the subprogram has dependencies in turn on other objects. The 'other objects' are indirect dependencies of the subprogram.

Direct Dependencies

A procedure or function might directly reference one of the following object types:

- Table
- View
- Sequence
- Procedure
- Function

Indirect Dependencies

If a procedure or function references a view, procedure or function that directly references one of the following object types, there is an indirect dependency:

- Table
- View
- Sequence
- Procedure
- Function

Describe dependent objects and referenced objects

- **Dependent Object** -- Any object in the database that references one or more other objects as part of its definition is a dependent object.
- **Referenced Object** -- Any object that is referenced in the definition of another database object is referred to as a referenced object.

A subprogram may either directly or indirectly reference a table, view, procedure, function, sequence, or packaged functions, procedures, types, etc.

- **Direct Dependency** – Object A references Object B. Object A has a direct dependency on Object B.
- **Indirect Dependency** -- Object A references Object B. Object B references Object C. Object A has a direct dependency on Object B and an indirect dependency on Object C.

For example, a procedure or function with a direct dependency on a view has an indirect dependency on any tables in the view's definition. Likewise a subprogram with a direct dependency on a procedure is indirectly dependent on any objects that procedure references. A change to the objects that are indirectly dependent can cause the direct dependent to become invalid, and therefore the subprogram itself will become invalid. This is cascading invalidation.

If an object is not valid when it is referenced, it must be validated before being used. Validation occurs automatically when an object is referenced. When an object is invalidated, on the next access, the compiler will attempt to recompile. If it recompiles without errors, it is revalidated; otherwise, it will remain invalid. When the definition of a referenced object is changed, this may prevent dependent objects from being able to recompile. For example, if a table is dropped, then any view that queries that table can no longer function. Any procedure referencing that view will be unable to compile successfully.

View dependency information in the dictionary views

The USER_DEPENDENCIES can be queried to display all the direct dependencies on an object in your schema. The dependent objects in this table will be only ones in your schema, but the referenced objects can be in any schema. The ALL_DEPENDENCIES and DBA_DEPENDENCIES views display the same information for all dependent objects to which you have access, and all dependent objects in the database respectively. Each has an OWNER column to reference the owner of the object. None of these views will display indirect dependencies. These can be obtained through the use of the UTLDTREE.SQL script which will be discussed in the next section. The following two queries display information about the dependencies that the OCPGURU schema has on the HR schema:

```
SELECT  name, referenced_name, referenced_type
FROM    user_dependencies
WHERE   type = 'PROCEDURE'
AND     referenced_owner = 'HR'

NAME             REFERENCED_NAME  REFERENCED_TYPE
---------------  ---------------  ---------------
GET_EMPLOYEE     EMPLOYEES        TABLE
```

```
EMP_YEARS          EMPLOYEES           TABLE
EMPS_DS            EMPLOYEES           TABLE


SELECT DISTINCT type, referenced_name, referenced_type
FROM   user_dependencies
WHERE  referenced_owner = 'HR'

TYPE             REFERENCED_NAME      REFERENCED_TYPE
-------------    ------------------   ----------------
SYNONYM          DEPARTMENTS          TABLE
PACKAGE BODY     EMPLOYEES            TABLE
PROCEDURE        EMPLOYEES            TABLE
```

Describe how the UTLDTREE script is used

The UTLDTREE.SQL script file creates two additional views (DEPTREE and IDEPTREE), and a procedure (DEPTREE_FILL). These can be used to provide a much easier means for finding indirect dependencies. Once this script file has been run in your schema, you can execute the DEPTREE_FILL procedure against an object that might be referenced by one or more objects (either directly or indirectly). The procedure will locate all objects that have a dependency on the identified object. The results can be viewed in by querying the DEPTREE or IDEPTREE views created by the script. The syntax to run the DEPTREE_FILL procedure is:

```
EXECUTE deptree_fill ('object_type', 'object_owner',
'object_name')
```

The two views created by the script are:

DEPTREE

This view, created by utldtree.sql, contains information on the object dependency tree. For user SYS, this view displays shared cursors (and only shared cursors) that depend on the object. For all other users, it displays objects other than shared cursors. Other users can access SYS.DEPTREE for information on shared cursors. The columns are:

- **NESTED_LEVEL** -- Nesting level in the dependency tree
- **TYPE** -- Object type
- **OWNER** -- Object owner
- **NAME** -- Object name
- **SEQ#** -- Sequence number in the dependency tree. Used for ordering queries.

IDEPTREE

This view, created by utldtree.sql, lists the indented dependency tree. It is a pre-sorted, pretty-print version of DEPTREE. The columns are:

- **NESTED_LEVEL** -- Nesting level in the dependency tree
- **TYPE** -- Object type
- **OWNER** -- Object owner
- **NAME** -- Object name

Describe how the IDEPTREE and DEPTREE views are used

The two views created by the UTLDTREE.SQL script are used to display the direct and indirect dependencies on a given object. This can help you to determine what objects in the database might be invalidated if you make changes to a particular object. If one or more objects might be invalidated, you might decide not to alter the object, or to alter it after hours, or simply to recompile those objects explicitly after changing the referenced object.

The example below creates a function and a procedure that references it. The DIRECT_REFERENCE function references the view EMPLOYEES_DEPT_V. The procedure DEPENDEDNT_PROC calls the function (and therefore references it). The procedure then has a direct dependency on the function, and an indirect dependency on the view.

The results from the queries against DEPTREE and IDEPTREE show this (as expected):

```
CREATE FUNCTION direct_reference
RETURN VARCHAR2
AS
  v_retval    VARCHAR2(20);
BEGIN
  SELECT last_name
  INTO   v_retval
  FROM   employees_dept_v
  WHERE  employee_id = 116;

  RETURN v_retval;
END direct_reference;

CREATE PROCEDURE dependent_proc
AS
  v_retval    VARCHAR2(20);
BEGIN
  v_retval := direct_reference;
END dependent_proc;


EXECUTE deptree_fill('VIEW', 'OCPGURU', 'EMPLOYEES_DEPT_V');
anonymous block completed


SELECT * FROM deptree;

NESTED_LEVEL TYPE         SCHEMA       NAME                    SEQ#
------------ -----------  -----------  --------------------    ----
           1 FUNCTION     OCPGURU      DIRECT_REFERENCE           2
           2 PROCEDURE    OCPGURU      DEPENDENT_PROC             3
           0 VIEW         OCPGURU      EMPLOYEES_DEPT_V           0


SELECT * FROM ideptree;

DEPENDENCIES
------------------------------------
FUNCTION OCPGURU.DIRECT_REFERENCE
PROCEDURE OCPGURU.DEPENDENT_PROC
VIEW OCPGURU.EMPLOYEES_DEPT_V
```

Describe a remote dependency

Remote dependency management is how the Oracle Database manages dependencies in distributed environments. For example, in a distributed database, a local view's defining query can reference a remote table. Alternately, a local procedure might call a remote function. Oracle does not manage dependencies among remote schema objects other than local-procedure-to-remote-procedure dependencies.

A local dependency involves two objects on the same database node. Object A on Database A references Object B on Database A. A remote dependency involves two objects on different database nodes. Object A on Database A references Object B on Database B. Because database A does not have control over Object B, the normal methods of verifying that the dependent object has not changed are not possible.

List how remote dependencies are governed

Remote dependencies among stored procedures are managed using either time-stamp checking or signature checking. The initialization parameter REMOTE_DEPENDENCIES_MODE determines which of the two will be used. The two possible values of this parameter are:

- **TIMESTAMP** -- Only timestamps are used to resolve dependencies (unless dynamically overridden).
- **SIGNATURE** -- Signatures are used to resolve dependencies (unless dynamically overridden).

Timestamp Model

When using the time-stamp model, whenever a procedure is compiled or recompiled, its time stamp is recorded in the data dictionary. The time stamp indicates when the procedure is created, altered, or replaced. The compilation code of the procedure also contains information about each referenced remote procedure. This data includes the schema, package name, procedure name, and time stamp.

Every time a dependent procedure is invoked, the database compares the remote time stamps recorded at compile time with the current time stamps of all remotely referenced procedures. If the timestamps match, then the local and remote procedures run successfully. However, if they do not match, then the local procedure is invalidated and an error is returned to the calling environment. In addition, any other local procedures that depend on that same remote procedure will also be invalidated.

If the local dependant procedure with a remote dependency is in an INVALID status when an attempt is made to execute it, Oracle will attempt to recompile it. If the remote procedure is valid, the local subprogram will successfully recompile and the current timestamp of the remote subprogram will be stored in the local subprogram's object code. To avoid errors caused by remote invalidations, you should always manually recompile any local subprograms with remote dependencies after the remote subprogram has been recompiled.

Signature Model

The alternative to the timestamp model is signature checking using RPC signatures. The RPC signature capability is used only for remote dependencies and has no effect on or relevance to local dependencies. When using this model, the RPC signature of a procedure contains information about the following items:

- The name of the unit (the package, procedure, or function name).
- The types of each of the parameters of the subprogram.
- The modes of the parameters (IN, OUT, IN OUT).
- The number of parameters.
- The type of the return value for a function.

When the database is set to make use of the RPC signature dependency model, an invalidation of the dependent unit will occur if the RPC signature of the remote program has been changed in an incompatible manner. A program unit can be a package, stored procedure, stored function, or trigger.

Describe when a remote dependency is unsuccessfully recompiled

Recompiling local objects with remote dependencies will be unsuccessful in the following situations:

- The arguments of a referenced procedure have been modified.
- The data type of a referenced column has been altered.
- The referenced object has been dropped, or renamed, or is invalid.
- A referenced view has been altered and has different columns.

Describe when a remote dependency is successfully recompiled

Recompiling local objects with remote dependencies will be successful in the following situations:

- The table being referenced has additional columns.
- Referenced columns have the same data types.
- The body of a PL/SQL procedure has been changed but recompiled successfully.

List how to minimize dependency failures

There are several steps you can take to minimize the number of dependency failures in your database:

- Make use of the %ROWTYPE attribute when declaring records.
- Make use of the %TYPE attribute when declaring variables.
- Use the SELECT * notation when querying tables
- Provide a column list when using INSERT statements

Study Guide for 1Z0-147

ABOUT THE AUTHOR

Matthew Morris is an Oracle Database Administrator and Developer currently employed as a Database Engineer with Computer Sciences Corporation. Matthew has worked with the Oracle database since 1996 when he worked in the RDBMS support team for Oracle Support Services. Employed with Oracle for over eleven years in support and development positions, Matthew was an early adopter of the Oracle Certified Professional program. He was one of the first one hundred Oracle Certified Database Administrators (version 7.3) and in the first hundred to become an Oracle Certified Forms Developer. In the years since, he has upgraded his Database Administrator certification for releases 8i, 9i, 10G and 11G, added the Application Express and SQL Expert certifications, and the PL/SQL Developer Certified Associate certification. Outside of Oracle, he has CompTIA certifications in Linux+ and Security+.

Made in the USA
Lexington, KY
18 February 2013